CHAMBERS

Effective
Grammar

CHAMBERS
An imprint of Chambers Harrap Publishers Ltd
7 Hopetoun Crescent
Edinburgh EH7 4AY

This (second) edition published by Chambers Harrap Publishers Ltd 2005
Previous edition published as *Chambers Guide to Effective Grammar* 1999
Copyright © Chambers Harrap Publishers Ltd 2005

A CIP catalogue record for this book is available from the British Library.

ISBN 0550 10140 3

Designed and typeset by Chambers Harrap Publishers Ltd, Edinburgh
Printed and bound in Spain by Graphy Cems

CONTRIBUTORS

Editors
Gill Francis
Kay Cullen

Series Editor
Elaine O'Donoghue

Publishing Manager
Patrick White

Prepress Manager
Sharon McTeir

Prepress Controller
Kirsteen Wright

CONTENTS

Introduction

Nowadays, many of us are afraid of grammar and are unconfident about their knowledge of it. This handy volume is intended to alleviate that fear and provide the basics of everyday grammar in a clear and useful way.

What exactly is grammar? There are many definitions, but for our purposes it is the part of language study which describes and explains the rules governing the arrangement of words into sentences, together with the description and explanation of how words are formed.

Why do we need grammar? It is essential if we want to use language precisely and communicate effectively. Sloppy or incorrect grammar can mar a written document, whether a report, job application or presentation, and leave a bad impression on the reader. A strong foundation in grammar is also useful when learning other languages.

The first chapter outlines why the book is structured in the way it is, from the building blocks of nouns and verbs to complex sentences and clauses. Jargon is avoided as much as possible but essential terms are explained clearly in the practical glossary at the front.

All points are illustrated with copious examples. Concise checklists summarize the main points of the chapter, and information boxes and usage boxes throughout the book highlight helpful facts and tips. At the end of most chapters there is an opportunity to put your knowledge into practice – solutions are provided after the final chapter.

INTRODUCTION

This guide is structured so that it can be read from chapter to chapter, thus building up a step-by-step knowledge of the fundamentals of English grammar. However, with its comprehensive index it is also envisaged as a useful reference tool which no desk can be without.

Other Desktop Guides are: *Perfect Punctuation*, *Letter Writing* and *Common Errors*. The *Chambers Good Writing Guide* provides useful tips on topics such as style, sensitive language and proofreading your own work.

Glossary

abstract noun a noun which refers to a quality, idea or experience that has no physical existence, and cannot be touched or seen
▸ see also **concrete noun**

active voice a verb in the active voice is one whose subject performs the action of the verb, as in *the dog bit the boy*
▸ see also **passive voice**

adjective a word that provides more information about a noun, eg *blue*, *several*

adjective group a word or group of words that functions as the complement or object complement of a clause. It consists of a head adjective that may be preceded by one or more adverbs. The head may be followed by a prepositional phrase, a *that*-clause or a *to*-infinitive clause, as in *the banjo is easy to learn*

adjunct the element in a clause that gives information about when, how, where, why or in what circumstances something happens, eg *I saw her on Tuesday*

adverb a word that gives information about when, how, where, why or in what circumstances something happens or is done, eg *almost*, *quickly*

adverb group a word or group of words that functions to give information about when, how, where, why or in what circumstances something happens or is done. It consists of a head adverb which may be preceded by a grading adverb such as *very*, eg *He left very quickly*.

adverb of degree another term for a **grading adverb**

adverbial clause an umbrella term for the nine types of subordinate clause that answer questions like 'Why?', 'When?', 'Where?' etc

GLOSSARY

affix a prefix, a group of letters added to the beginning of the word, such as *un-* or *de-*, or a suffix, a group of letters added to the end of a word, such as *-ness* or *-ship*

attributive the position of an adjective when it comes before a noun, or the adjective itself, eg *the red car*

auxiliary verb the verbs *be*, *do* and *have*, which are combined with main verbs to form compound tenses, eg *He has gone*

bare infinitive the base form of a verb used in some structures, eg *I saw him go*

base form the form of a verb on which other forms are based, such as *stop* or *enter*

broad negative an adverb such as *barely* or *hardly*, which is nearly negative in meaning

cardinal number a number that indicates quantity, eg *one*, *five*, *32*

central adjective an adjective such as *busy* or *happy*, which can be used in either the attributive or the predicative position, eg *The scarf is green*; *the green scarf*

clause a sequence of words that includes a verb. Clauses may be main or subordinate, finite or non-finite

cleft sentence a sentence that has been split into two clauses so that one part of the sentence is given greater emphasis, eg *It was Jim who arrived first*

closed word class a word class which contains a fixed number of words that cannot be added to. Pronouns, determiners, prepositions and conjunctions are all closed word classes
▸ see also **open word class**

collective noun a noun that refers to a group of people or things, such as *family* or *audience*. It can be used with either a singular or a plural verb

common noun any noun that is not a proper noun, eg *table*, *book*

comparative the form of a graded adjective or adverb that is used for saying that someone or something has more or less of a quality than someone or something else, or than before. It is formed by adding the ending *-er* to a word or by adding the words *more* or *less*, eg *taller*, *less important*

complement the element in a clause that describes or identifies the subject, eg *That is <u>the question</u>*

complex sentence a sentence that consists of a main clause and one or more subordinate clauses, eg *You'll make it on time if you leave now*

compound adjective an adjective that consists of two or more words, such as *kind-hearted* or *present-day*

compound adverb an adverb that consists of two or more words, such as *cold-bloodedly* or *good-naturedly*

compounding the process of linking two or more words to create a new compound word, eg *income tax*, *water-ski*

compound noun a noun that consists of two or more words, such as *make-up* or *three-line whip*

compound sentence a sentence that consists of two or more main clauses linked by co-ordinating conjunctions, eg *Sandy played guitar and Hamish sang*

compound tense a tense that shows how an action or event is to be regarded with respect to time: whether it is complete or still in progress at the time of speaking or at the time being referred to, eg *I <u>have</u> already <u>eaten</u>*; *He <u>had left</u> by then*

concessive clause a subordinate clause that contrasts with a main clause in some way, eg *He was happy, <u>despite finishing last</u>*

concrete noun a noun which refers to something that has a real physical existence and can be touched or seen

▶ see also **abstract noun**

conditional clause a subordinate clause used to talk about a possible situation and often introduced by the subordinating conjunction *if*

GLOSSARY

conjunction a word that links words, groups or clauses, eg *and*

co-ordinating conjunction a conjunction, such as *and* or *but*, that links words, groups or clauses of equal status

co-ordination the linking of words, groups or clauses of equal status within a sentence

count noun a noun that can be counted. It can have both a singular and a plural form

definite article the word *the*

demonstrative determiner the determiners *this*, *that*, *these* and *those*, which are used before nouns to refer to relative position in space or time

demonstrative pronoun the pronouns *this*, *that*, *these* and *those*, which are used on their own to refer to relative position in space or time

derivation the process of adding an affix to a word to create a new word, eg <u>dis</u>like, like<u>ness</u>

determiner a word such as *the* or *some* that goes before a noun and indicates whether you are referring to a particular thing or something of a particular type

direct object the element in a clause that indicates the person or thing affected by an action or process, eg *He kissed <u>her</u>*

ditransitive verb a verb that has a direct object and can also have an indirect object. In *He buys her flowers every day*, the direct object is *flowers* and the indirect object is *her*. *Buy* is a ditransitive verb

dummy subject the word *it* when it has no meaning but is used as the subject of a clause in a sentence, eg *It is raining*

-ed form the base form of a regular verb with *-ed* added, used for the past participle and to form the past tense, eg *laughed*

ellipsis the process of omitting parts of a clause when otherwise they would be repeated, eg *They were laughing and (they were) singing*

emphasizing adjective another term for **intensifying adjective**

ergative verb a verb that can be used transitively to focus on the person who performs an action or intransitively to focus on the thing affected by an action, as in *he broke the window*; *the window broke*

exclamative determiner the words *what* and *such* which are used in exclamations such as *what a beautiful day!*

finite verb group a verb group that shows tense, number, person and how an action is to be regarded in time, eg *I go to school every day*

▸ see also **non-finite verb group**

finite clause a clause containing a finite verb group

▸ see also **non-finite clause**

focusing adverb an adverb that is used to focus on the main thing involved in a situation, eg *chiefly*, *primarily*, *solely*

general determiner an umbrella term for the indefinite article *a* or *an* and other determiners such as *some* and *each*

graded adjective/adverb an adjective or adverb that has comparative and superlative forms and can be modified by a grading adverb such as *very*, eg *sad*, *quickly*

▸ see also **ungraded adjective/adverb**

grading adverb an adverb such as *very* or *fairly* that is used in front of an adjective or adverb to indicate degree

head the most important word in a group. In the noun group *a nice girl*, *girl* is the head

helping verb another term for **auxiliary verb**

imperative one of the moods of a verb group, used in commands and instructions, eg *Come here! Do not enter!*

indefinite article the words *a* and *an*

indefinite pronoun a pronoun such as *anyone* or *everything*, which is used to refer to people or things without saying who or which they are

indicative one of the moods of a verb group, used for making statements, eg *He* <u>went</u> *home; She* <u>isn't</u> *here*

indirect object the element in a clause which indicates the person who is (or people who are) the receiver(s) of an action or process, eg *He gave* <u>his uncle</u> *the letter*

infinitive an umbrella term for the bare infinitive and the *to*-infinitive

intensifying adjective an adjective such as *absolute* or *complete*, which is used before a noun to emphasize it

interjection a word class consisting of words and short phrases conveying some sort of emotion, such as *Ouch!* or *Wow!*

-ing form the base form of a verb with *-ing* added, used to form the present participle and the progressive tenses

interrogative one of the moods of the verb group, used for asking questions, eg *Have you got your keys?*

interrogative determiner the determiners *which*, *what* and *whose*, which are used before nouns to ask questions

interrogative pronoun a pronoun such as *who* or *what*, which are used on their own to ask questions

intransitive verb a verb that does not have an object, such as *walk*

irregular verb a verb that does not regularly form the past tense and past participle by adding *-ed*, such as *fight* or *sleep*
▸ see also **regular verb**

lexical verb another term for **main verb**

link verb a verb such as *be* or *seem*, which is used to talk about what someone or something is or seems to be

linking adjunct an adverb group or a prepositional phrase that connects one clause or sentence with another, eg *beforehand*, *finally*, *on the contrary*, *therefore*

main clause a clause that is grammatically independent, eg *Wherever I go, she follows me*

main verb the most important verb in a clause, which may be supported by one or more auxiliary verbs

mass noun a noun that is both count and uncount. It refers to substances such as *detergent*, where you can also talk about a type or brand of the substance, in which case you can say *a detergent* or *detergents*

modal auxiliary a word such as *can* or *should*, used for expressing ability, obligation etc

mood one of the forms of a verb group. There are four moods: indicative, interrogative, imperative and subjunctive

non-finite verb group a verb group that does not show tense, aspect, number or person, eg *Weather permitting we will start at 6pm*
▶ see also **finite verb group**

non-finite clause a clause that does not contain a finite verb group, eg *He looked at her as though puzzled*
▶ see also **finite clause**

noun a word used to name people, places, things, ideas etc, eg *cat*, *Edinburgh*

noun clause a clause such as *what I want* that can function as the subject, object, or complement of another clause

noun group a word or group of words that functions as the subject, object or complement of a clause. It consists of a head noun and may also contain determiners, adjectives, prepositional phrases, or defining relative clauses, eg *He broke those crystal wine glasses that I bought last week*

number a cardinal number, ordinal number or fraction, which may be written using figures or letters

object complement the element in a clause that is used to say more about the direct object. In *they elected him president*, *president* is the object complement

open word class a word class that can and does admit new words. Nouns, verbs, adjectives and adverbs are all open word classes

▸ see also **closed word class**

ordinal a type of number that indicates a position in a series, eg *first*, *second*, *third*, *31st*

participial adjective the present or past participle of a verb used as an adjective, such as *flying glass* or *frozen peas*

particle an adverb or a preposition that goes after a main verb to make a phrasal verb such as *take back* or *give in*

part of speech see **word class**

passive voice a verb in the passive voice is one whose subject is the person or thing that an action is done to, as in *the boy was bitten by the dog*

▸ see also **active voice**

past participle the base form of a regular verb with *-ed* added. The past participles of irregular verbs may be different, such as *stolen* or *given*

personal pronoun a pronoun which refers to people or things, such as *he* or *them*

phrasal modal a modal auxiliary that consists of more than one word, eg *be able to*, *be bound to*, *would rather*

phrasal verb a verb made up of a main verb and a preposition or adverb, such as *look after*, *put up with* or *bring up*

plural noun a noun that is always plural, such as *belongings* or *surroundings*

polar question another term for a **yes/no question**

post-determiner a kind of adjective, such as *same* or *usual*, that comes after another determiner and before any other adjectives in a noun group, eg *the same old story*

possessive determiner a determiner such as *my* or *his*, which shows who something belongs to or is associated with

possessive pronoun a pronoun such as *mine* or *yours*, which shows who or what something belongs to or is associated with

pre-determiner a determiner such as *double* or *half* that comes before another determiner, eg <u>*All*</u> *the trees are bare*

predicate the verb element in a clause, consisting of a head verb and its associated auxiliaries, eg *the cup* <u>*is on the table*</u>

predicative the position of an adjective when it comes after a link verb, or the adjective itself, eg *the car is* <u>*red*</u>

prefix one or more letters, such as *un-* or *de-*, added to the beginning or a word to create a new word, such as <u>*co*</u>*-star* or <u>*dis*</u>*like*

preposition a word such as *in* or *at*, which allow us to talk about place, time, and other relationships between people, things or situations

prepositional object a noun group that follows a preposition, eg *on* <u>*the table*</u>

prepositional phrase a preposition followed by a noun group, eg *on the table*

present participle the base form of a verb with *-ing* added

pronoun a word such as *me* or *they* that can be substituted for a noun group

proper noun a name given to a particular person, place or thing, typically starting with a capital letter, eg *Paris*, *Tom*

quantifier a word used for talking about a quantity of people or things, which is followed by *of*, eg <u>*lots*</u> *of people*

reciprocal pronoun the pronouns *each other* and *one another*

reciprocal verb a verb that describes an action in which two or more people or groups do the same thing to each other. It can have a plural or singular subject, as in *we quarrelled*; *I quarrelled with her*

GLOSSARY

reflexive pronoun a pronoun such as *myself* or *ourselves*, which is used to talk about oneself

regular verb a verb that adds *-ed* to its past tense and past participle forms, such as *shout* and *jump*

▶ see also **irregular verb**

relative pronoun a pronoun such as *who* or *that*, which is used to introduce a relative clause

relative clause a clause that is usually introduced by a relative pronoun, which identifies or gives more information about someone or something, eg *The book that you wanted is over there*

-s form the base form of a verb with an *s* added, used for the third person simple present tense, eg *Sam speaks French*

sentence a sequence of words, or sometimes a single word, which begins with a capital letter and ends with a full stop, question mark or exclamation mark

sentence adjunct an adverb group or prepositional phrase that modifies a whole clause or sentence, eg *quite surprisingly*, *frankly*, *unfortunately*

semi-modal the verbs *dare* and *need*, which sometimes function like modal auxiliaries and sometimes like ordinary verbs

simple sentence a sentence consisting of only one clause, eg *It's very late*

simple tense the simple present and the simple past tense, eg *I work in the City*; *He arrived yesterday*

singular noun a noun that is used with a determiner and has no plural form, such as *gloom* and *profusion*

specific determiner an umbrella term for the definite article *the*, demonstrative determiners such as *this* and *that*, and possessive determiners such as *your* and *their*

subject the element in a clause that indicates the person or thing that is responsible for an action or process. It determines the form of a verb. In *he kissed her*, *he* is the subject

subjunctive one of the moods of a verb group, sometimes used when talking about hypothetical situations or requests, eg *I would leave now if I were you*

subordinate clause a clause that is grammatically dependent on a main clause or another subordinate clause, eg *He left as soon as it stopped raining*

subordinating conjunction a conjunction such as *because* or *whereas*, which links a subordinate clause to a main clause or another subordinate clause

suffix one or more letters added to the end of a word to create a new word, eg *-ness* or *-ship*

superlative the form of a graded adjective or adverb that is used for saying that someone or something has more or less of a quality than anyone or anything else. It is formed by adding the ending *-est* to a word or by adding *the most* or *the least*, eg *happiest*, *the most important*

tag question a short question added to the end of a statement, which you use to elicit agreement from your hearer, eg *She isn't laughing, is she?*

tense a particular form or set of verb forms that show at what time an action or process takes place, and whether it is complete or incomplete. Tenses are either simple or compound

that-clause a clause beginning with the word *that*

to-infinitive clause a clause beginning with a *to*-infinitive, eg *I'm ready to leave now*

transitive verb a verb that has an object, such as *hit*, eg *He fixed the window*

uncount noun a noun that refers to things that cannot be counted, such as *water* or *love*

GLOSSARY

ungraded adjective/adverb an adjective or adverb that has no comparative or superlative forms and cannot be modified by a grading adverb such as *very*, eg *electric* or *unique*

▸ see also **graded adjective/adverb**

verb a word that expresses actions, communication, mental processes and states of being, eg *have*, *think* or *see*

verb group a word or group of words that functions as the verb element of a clause. It consists of a main verb and may also contain one or more auxiliaries, eg *The children are playing outside*; *The event is funded by the council*

voice a verb group may be in the active or the passive voice

wh-word an umbrella term for the pronouns, determiners and adverbs used in questions, such as *where* or *who*

word class a group of words with a particular grammatical function. In this book we describe ten word classes: nouns, verbs, adjectives, adverbs, pronouns, determiners, prepositions, conjunctions, numerals and interjections.

yes/no question a question for which the expected answer is either 'yes' or 'no', eg *Are you hungry?*

Word classes or parts of speech

As a first step in the study of grammar, it is logical to begin with the basic building blocks of language: individual words. Words are units of meaning made up of combinations of **letters**, which may be vowels or consonants. **Vowels** are the letters *a*, *e*, *i*, *o*, *u*. **Consonants** are the letters *b*, *c*, *d*, *f*, *g*, *h*, *j*, *k*, *l*, *m*, *n*, *p*, *q*, *r*, *s*, *t*, *v*, *w*, *x*, *y*, *z*.

We usually group words into **word classes**, or **parts of speech**. The class that a word falls into depends partly on its form and function. For example, a **noun** referring to something that you can count (a **count noun**) often ends in *s* or *es*, and an **adverb** often ends in *ly*, which are questions of form. Nouns often name things, and adverbs often refer to the way in which something is done, which are to do with function. A **verb** has a variety of forms for different tenses, and its main functions are to express doing, saying, thinking and being.

The environment of a word also helps us to decide its class. For example, you often see a **determiner** such as *a*, *an*, or *this* before a singular count noun, or *some* or *those* before a plural count noun. Nouns are often preceded by **adjectives** (*a big house*) or by other nouns (*a language school*). Similarly, an adjective may be preceded by *very*, *more* or *less*, and may be followed by *than*.

Many words belong to more than one word class. For example, the word *can* is both a noun and a verb; the word *his* is a **pronoun** and a **possessive determiner**; the word *light* is a noun, a verb and an adjective, and the word *fast* is a noun, a verb, an adjective and an adverb. Some words fall into even more classes: for example, it is difficult to work out all the different classes of very frequent words like *both*, *all* and *what*.

In addition, it is not always easy to decide on the class of a particular word, because the boundaries can be fuzzy. For example, which word class or classes does the common little word *worth* belong to? In sentences like *The town is worth a visit*, *worth* behaves very much like a **preposition**, in that it introduces a noun (compare *on a visit*; *for a visit*). But here the grammatical environment and the meaning are at odds, because *worth* seems to have an adjective-like meaning in spite of its preposition-like behaviour. Then in sentences like *I bought a pound's worth of chocolates*, it seems to belong to another completely different class, but one that is very hard to pin down. All this goes to show that word class is not set in stone; some words are very difficult to classify.

We often say that a particular word class is either **'open'** or **'closed'**. An open word class is one that will admit new words. Most new words, or **neologisms**, are nouns or verbs: new nouns are required when we need to assign a name to a new phenomenon, process or invention such as *Internet* or *DVD*. English readily allows new verbs and phrasal verbs to be created from existing nouns (eg the verb *network* from the noun *network*, and the phrasal verb *pig out* from the noun *pig*). Furthermore, there is the ongoing process of adopting into English new words from other languages, such as *cappuccino* or *sushi*.

A closed word class is one that contains a fixed number of words that cannot be added to. The word class of prepositions, for example, is a closed class. We can list them: *in*, *by*, *from*, *on*, *over* and so on. It is quite a long list, but it is fixed and finite.

In this book, words are dealt with class by class. Earlier chapters deal with major word classes and the remaining chapters deal with more minor word classes.

Nouns and noun groups

Nouns are used to identify people or things. Nouns are an open class: there are many thousands of them and the class can be added to as we assign names to things that are new to our experience of the world.

Verbs and phrasal verbs

Verbs are used to say what someone or something does, what happens to them or what they are. Verbs are an open class. New ones frequently appear in English, often created from existing English nouns. This chapter also describes the combinations known as **phrasal verbs** (like *look after* and *bring up*), which function grammatically as verbs even though one or more of their constituent words is a **particle**, like *after* or *up*.

Verb tenses

This chapter lists and exemplifies the tenses that a verb group can have.

More about verb groups

This chapter gives more information about verb groups: active and passive, finite and non-finite, and mood.

Adjectives and adjective groups

Adjectives are used to describe things and people or give information about them. Adjectives are an open class.

Adverbs, adverb groups and adjuncts

Adverbs are used to give information about when, how, where, why or in what circumstances something happens. Adverbs are an open class. This chapter also deals with adjuncts, which are the part of the clause that adverb groups often function as.

Pronouns

Pronouns are used to stand in for nouns: instead of saying *my father*, you can say *he*. Pronouns are a closed class. For example, the **personal pronouns** used as **subjects** in modern English are *I*, *you*, *he*, *she*, *it*, *we* and *they*, and this list cannot be added to. Only the pronouns used in modern English are discussed in this chapter, though the class also includes older forms, such as *thee* and *thine*.

Determiners

Determiners are used in front of nouns to show whether you are referring to a specific thing or to something of a particular type: *the dog* refers to a particular dog, while *a dog* is less specific. Determiners are a closed class, for example, there are only three **articles**, *a*, *an* and *the*, and the list cannot be added to.

Prepositions and prepositional phrases

Prepositions, like *in*, *on* and *to* are used to refer to position or movement, as well as a variety of other meanings. Prepositions are a closed class.

Conjunctions

Conjunctions, like *and*, *because* and *if* are used to link words and parts of clauses or sentences together. Conjunctions are a closed class.

Numbers

Numbers are used to count people and things. There are three basic types of number: cardinal numbers, ordinal numbers and fractions. Numbers are a closed class in that even the largest numbers are made up of only ten digits.

Other chapters deal with topics such as clauses, sentences and word formation.

Parts of the clause

A clause is a sequence of words that includes a verb. We will begin by introducing the basic elements that go to making up a clause, since these are terms that we will be using throughout the book. A clause can have up to seven basic elements: a **subject**, a **predicate** or **verb**, a **direct object**, an **indirect object**, a **complement**, an **object complement** and one or more adjuncts. Of these, the only one that is essential is the verb, as in clauses like *Stop!* This is the shortest type of clause, and contains only a verb.

Clauses are dealt with in detail on pages 172–83.

The subject

The subject of a clause is the person or thing that is responsible for an action or process. It usually comes before the verb in statements, and after auxiliary verbs (eg *be*, *do* or *have*) in questions:

> *Cats are popular household pets.*

> *Do you like cats?*

The subject determines the form of the verb – whether it is singular or plural:

> *My cousin likes him.*

> *Women like him.*

A subject consists of a **noun group** as in the above examples, or of two or more **co-ordinated** noun groups (noun groups that are connected by a word like *and* or *or*):

> *Cats and dogs are popular household pets.*
>
> *Julie, Jane and I are off to see a film.*

The subject of a clause may also be the 'dummy subject' *it*. This is called the dummy subject because it has no meaning and is used simply because otherwise the sentence would have no subject:

> *It is rather cold in here.*
>
> *It is obvious that you are quite wrong.*

The subject may also consist of a **noun clause**, that is, a clause that is used instead of a noun group, and that can be replaced by a noun group:

> *What you need is a good shower.*
>
> *That he was jealous of me was becoming increasingly apparent.*

The latter type of clause is rare. You generally use *it* as the subject and put the real subject at the end of the clause:

> *It was becoming increasingly apparent that he was jealous of me.*

The predicate

The predicate is the verb element in a clause. It consists of a **verb group**, which may be a main verb on its own or a main verb with **auxiliaries** in front of it. It refers to what is happening in the clause:

> *Mary sang a song.*
>
> *The children are playing outside.*
>
> *You have been warned.*

The predicate may consist of two or more co-ordinated verb groups (verb groups that are connected by a word like *and* or *or*):

> *The baby was crying and coughing.*
>
> *We were eating, drinking and dancing all night.*

The direct object

The direct object usually refers to the person or thing affected by an action or process. It consists of a noun group or of two or more co-ordinated noun groups:

> *Cook the mushrooms until soft.*
>
> *They want to change the world.*
>
> *She can't drive a car.*
>
> *I saw Marie and Fred at the party.*
>
> *I want to address my colleagues, friends and relatives.*

The direct object may also consist of a noun clause, that is, a clause that is used instead of a noun group:

> *That's what I want.*
>
> *I understand that the factory will close soon.*

Note that many clauses do not have a direct object, because many verbs are **intransitive** (see page 39).

The indirect object

The indirect object refers to the person or people who are the receivers of an action. It may be someone who is given something, or for whom someone does something. It consists of a noun group, or of two or more co-ordinated noun groups. The indirect object comes before the direct object:

> I gave *my mother* some flowers.
>
> She knitted *him* a warm scarf.
>
> I realize that I owe *her* an apology.
>
> I lent *John and Alison* some money.

The complement

The complement is the element of the clause that describes or identifies the subject. It is used after **link verbs**, which are verbs used to talk about states of being, becoming, seeming etc (see page 40). It may be a noun group or two or more co-ordinated noun groups:

> That is *a very difficult question.*
>
> The police formed *a line* across the road.
>
> He became *an inspector* in 1995.
>
> She'll make *a good leader.*
>
> He was *a colleague and a friend.*

It may be an **adjective group** or two or more co-ordinated adjective groups:

> Cigarettes are *dangerous to your health.*
>
> I'm *afraid of him.*
>
> The sauce tastes *nice.*
>
> The baby looked *happy and healthy.*
>
> You seem *tired and stressed.*

Sometimes the complement is a **prepositional phrase**, that is, a phrase that consists of a preposition and a noun group:

> *I got into a panic.*
>
> *The cat is in the garden.*

The object complement

Some clauses can have a complement after their direct object. This is known as an object complement. It is used to say more about the direct object. It may be a noun group or two or more co-ordinated noun groups:

> *They appointed him chairman.*
>
> *Her critics called her a complete and utter failure.*
>
> *They named their children Colin and Angela.*

It may be an adjective group:

> *They called this book dangerous.*
>
> *You are driving me mad.*
>
> *I will hold you solely responsible.*

Adjuncts

Adjuncts give information about when, how, where, why or in what circumstances something happens. An adjunct is often an **adverb group**:

> *She worked quite quickly.*
>
> *He reported accurately on what he had seen.*
>
> *I'm afraid I played very badly.*

It may be a prepositional phrase:

> *I saw her in the afternoon.*
> *We had lasagne for dinner.*
> *They climbed up the hill.*

Occasionally adjuncts are noun groups:

> *She was born last April.*
> *He visited me yesterday.*

Unlike the other elements discussed above, there may be more than one adjunct in a clause. This one has three:

> *She was sleeping quietly in her bed this morning.*

For more information about adjuncts, see pages 102–7.

Checklist

A **clause** is a sequence of words that includes a verb. It can have up to seven elements:

1. **Subject**
- the person or thing that performs an action or process
- may be the dummy subject *it*

2. **Predicate**
- the verb element in a clause

3. **Direct object**
- the person or thing affected by an action or process

4. **Indirect object**
- the person who is (or people who are) the receiver(s) of an action

- comes before the direct object

5. Complement
- the element of the clause that describes or identifies the subject
- is used after link verbs such as *be* or *become*

6. Object complement
- is used to say more about the direct object

7. Adjunct
- gives information about the circumstances in which something happens

Grammar in practice

A In the following sentences, pick out the subjects, objects, complements and adjuncts:

1 *The prison had been built by the British early in the century.*

2 *Four thousand men and women were imprisoned here.*

3 *The lighthouse threw a wide blade of light across the horizon.*

4 *What was I doing there?*

5 *What I wanted was to get out of there.*

6 *An hour later we were sailing to Canton up the estuary of the Pearl River.*

7 *Canton is at once the flashiest and most traditional of the great cities.*

8 *Under the banyan trees, youths sell bracelets and pocket calculators.*

9 *One of these multi-tiered restaurants specializes in snakes.*

10 *Then he fell silent.*

B Pick out the indirect object in the following sentences:

1 *'Water', she whispered, and I gave her a sip.*

2 *He sends you his love.*

3 *We cooked the visitors a huge dinner.*

4 *He didn't even offer me his hand.*

5 *She asked me to bring her some tea.*

C Pick out the object complements in the following sentences:

1 *My children called him uncle and were always pleased to see him.*

2 *You can consider it a compliment.*

3 *He has proved himself a master of the art.*

4 *The bomb left nine people dead.*

5 *All people are born free and equal.*

Nouns and noun groups

A **noun** is used to identify a person or thing. The simplest definition of a noun is that it is a 'naming word' – this is the definition
with which most schoolchildren are familiar.

Noun groups

In use, nouns go together to form noun groups. Note that a noun
group can consist of just one noun. This is because a single noun
has the same function in a sentence as a noun group consisting
of two or more words. The most important word in a noun group
is called its **head**. In all the following noun groups, *computer* or
computers is the head:

> *computers*
>
> *my computer*
>
> *three computers*
>
> *an extremely small computer*
>
> *a new powerful computer*
>
> *a small but powerful computer*
>
> *the computer in my office*
>
> *the computer that I bought last week*

These examples show that the head can appear alone, or it can
be preceded by determiners like *the* or *my*, numbers, or adjectives. An adjective in its turn can be preceded by a **grading
adverb** like *extremely*. Sometimes more than one adjective is
used. In this case, there may be a **co-ordinating conjunction** like
but between the adjectives; this too is part of the noun group.

In the last two examples, a **prepositional phrase** and a **defining relative clause**, respectively, are considered to be part of the group. This is because they are crucial to the meaning of the head; they identify which computer you are talking about.

Some noun groups contain adjectives that occur after the head, eg *time immemorial*.

Noun groups are used as **subjects**, **complements**, **objects** and **object complements** in a clause. Occasionally they are used as **adjuncts**.

General characteristics of nouns

Nouns have some general characteristics and patterns, which help us to identify them.

- Nouns are often preceded by a determiner such as *a*, *the*, *few*, *many* or *this*, or by a number:

  a cinema

  an apple

  the girl

  few people

  every day

  many difficulties

  20 people

  the eighth day

- Nouns are often preceded by an adjective, or by more than one adjective:

  a fast car

  the tallest boy

  easy questions

cruel treatment

great achievements

a big red balloon

- Nouns are often used before other nouns, that is, they modify nouns:

  the car door

  a grammar book

  a computer table

  rugby players

  space travel

  the bedroom wall

- Nouns are often followed by a prepositional phrase to show what they relate to:

  my admiration for him

  his reply to your question

  reliance on a dictionary

  her relationship with me

  a quarrel between friends

  insurance against fire

- Nouns are often followed by a relative clause which identifies the person or thing you are talking about:

  the hospital that I visited last week

  the shoes you want

  the man I love

In all the above cases, nouns in use go with the other words to form noun groups.

Note also that nouns may end with an apostrophe and *s* (or, where the noun already ends in *s*, an apostrophe only) to indicate possession:

> *Andrew's* mother
>
> the *people's* choice
>
> *farmers'* incomes

Another characteristic of nouns is that they can often be identified by their endings. Typical endings are *-tion*, *-ment*, *-ism*, *-ist*, *-ness*, *-er* and *-or*, eg *satisfaction*, *contentment*, *atheism*, *sexist*, *happiness*, *butcher*, *instigator*.

Proper nouns and common nouns

All nouns can be divided into **proper nouns** and **common nouns**.

A proper noun (also sometimes called a **proper name**) is the name given to a particular person, place or thing that is unique, that is, there is usually only one of them. Proper nouns are usually signalled in writing by the use of an initial capital letter. A proper noun may consist of more than one word. The following are proper nouns:

- the names given to individual people. These may include a title, or may be a form of address, eg *Anthea*, *Michael Jones*, *Ms Jennifer Brown*, *Jesus Christ*, *Saint Christopher*, *the Queen*, *King John*, *Lord Jim*, *President Chirac*, *Inspector Philips*, *Aunt Jane*, *Mum*

- the names of places and geographical features, eg *Europe*, *Poland*, *British Columbia*, *Lincolnshire*, *Tuscany*, *Rome*, *the Highlands*, *the Mississippi*, *the Alps*, *the Gobi Desert*, *the Sea of Tranquillity*, *the Costa Blanca*, *the Pennine Way*, *Baker Street*

- a variety of things such as organizations, institutions, books, films, magazines, paintings, ships etc, eg *the BBC*, *the United Nations*, *Cheltenham College*, *the Bible*, *David Copperfield*, *The Return of the King*, *Nature*, *the Mona Lisa*, *the Queen Mary*

- the names of the months, days of the week and festivals, eg *March*, *October*, *Monday*, *Easter*, *Yom Kippur*, *Thanksgiving*, *Ramadan*, *Diwali*

Because they typically refer to someone or something unique, proper nouns do not usually have plural forms. However, a proper noun is occasionally used in the plural, especially where a number is specified:

> *'Which John do you mean? There are three Johns here.'*

> *She has given me socks four Christmases running.*

Similarly, when the name of a particular person is seen as epitomizing certain characteristics, and the name has come to be used in a general way to refer to any other person who has these characteristics, a plural is possible:

> *He said he left the job because all the managers were little Hitlers.*

> *His job is to spot all the potential Beckhams and sign them up for the team.*

> *A group of bronzed Adonises were playing volleyball on the beach.*

Any noun that does not name a particular person, place or thing is a common noun. Common nouns can be applied to more than one person, place or thing. Thus, while *Peter* and *Asia* are proper nouns, *man* and *continent* are common nouns.

Concrete nouns and abstract nouns

All common nouns can be divided into **concrete nouns** and **abstract nouns**.

A concrete noun is one that refers to something that has a real physical existence and can be touched or seen, eg *man*, *boy*, *sand*, *floor*, *soil*, *table*.

An abstract noun is one that refers to a quality, idea or experience that has no physical existence, eg *courage*, *fear*, *jealousy*, *strength*, *loyalty*, *humour*, *poverty*, *intelligence*. Many nouns (typically with the ending *-ing*) that refer to actions are also abstract nouns, eg *singing*, *dancing*, *fighting*, *performing*, *mimicking*.

Compound nouns

Compound nouns consist of two or more words. Some are written as separate words and some are written with hyphens, eg *musical instrument*, *guide dog*, *house sparrow*, *cane sugar*, *crocodile tears*, *three-line whip*, *counter-espionage*, *make-up*, *cross-reference*. Dictionaries differ as to what they enter as compound nouns, and they also differ in terms of whether a word is hyphenated or not; there are no hard and fast rules.

Many compound nouns that end in *-ing* refer to activities, eg *ice-skating*, *hang-gliding*, *horse-riding*, *power-boating*.

For more information about compound nouns, see pages 190–1.

The grammatical classification of nouns

Nouns can be divided into classes according to their grammatical behaviour, for example, whether they have plural forms, whether they can be preceded by *a* or *an*, whether they are always singular or always plural, and so on. Most nouns are either **count** or **uncount**.

Count nouns are also known as **countable nouns**. Uncount nouns can be called **non-count nouns** or **uncountable nouns**.

Count nouns

Count nouns refer to things that can be counted; if you can ask the question 'How many…?' about a noun, then it is a count noun. Count nouns have two forms, singular and plural. The plural form usually ends in *-s* or *-es*:

singular	plural
dog	*dogs*
monkey	*monkeys*
pursuer	*pursuers*
station	*stations*
metre	*metres*
bicycle	*bicycles*
noise	*noises*
story	*stories*

When they are singular, count nouns are always preceded by a determiner such as *a, an, the, another, each, every, neither*.

a day

an event

the sign

another disaster

neither house

each and every person

When they are plural, count nouns can be used without a determiner, eg *girls*, *eggs*, *cabbages*. They can also be used with determiners such as *the*, *both*, *a few*, *many*, *more*, *most* and *several*, or with numbers:

> the *children*
>
> both *occasions*
>
> a few *trees*
>
> many *weeks*
>
> more *problems*
>
> most *women*
>
> several *mistakes*
>
> two *solutions*
>
> a thousand *people*
>
> 35 *pieces*

Uncount nouns

Uncount nouns refer to substances such as *water* and *sand*, qualities such as *beauty* and *tolerance*, feelings such as *love* and *disgust*, abstract concepts such as *truth* and *experience*, types of activity such as *swimming* and *sailing*, and things like *luggage* and *furniture*. All these are things that are not normally counted or considered to be individual items.

Uncount nouns do not have a plural form, and are used with a singular verb. They are not used with numbers, and they do not need determiners, but are often used with a determiner such as *the* or *my*:

> He's got *flu*.
>
> The *milk* hasn't been delivered yet.
>
> *Milk* is good for you.

The furniture is Victorian.

Take my advice.

His disgust was obvious.

Skating is fun.

Most uncount nouns may be used with the determiners *much* and *little*, but not with the determiners *many* or *few*. It is also often possible to refer to a certain amount of an uncount noun using *some*, *any*, *a little*, *a great deal of*, etc:

I didn't have much homework.

He worked with little enthusiasm.

There is a great deal of traffic.

Is there any news?

I've only got a little luggage.

Notice that when certain uncount nouns are preceded by adjectives, or followed by prepositional phrases or relative clauses, they can be used with *a* or *an*, as in:

a great affection

an overriding fear

a formidable knowledge

an anxiety about the future

a happiness that I didn't deserve

However, there are some uncount nouns, like *advice*, *information* and *furniture*, that can never be used with *a* or *an*.

Count and uncount nouns

Many nouns have both count and uncount senses:

uncount	count
a great deal of *activity*	one of my favourite *activities*
a trench of great *depth*	the *depths* of despair
broken *glass*	two *glasses* of water
He was deep in *thought*.	I've just had a *thought*.

Many nouns are both count and uncount in the same sense, that is, they can be used with or without a determiner, and they have a plural form:

uncount	count
Injustice is everywhere.	He did me an *injustice*; the *injustices* of world poverty
He's not afraid of *death*.	an early *death*; It causes many *deaths*.
economic *hardship*	a terrible *hardship*; the *hard-ships* of life
delicious *cake*	a nice *cake*; lots of *cakes*
refreshing *lemonade*	a *lemonade*, three *lemonades*

There are several typically count nouns that behave like uncount nouns when they are used after determiners like *much*, *some*, *little*, *no* and *any*:

> *There isn't much point in asking him.*

> *She had little reason to stay.*

> *I have some idea of the implications.*

> *There is no difference between them.*

Some nouns that are both count and uncount are known as **mass nouns**. These nouns behave like uncount nouns when they refer to a substance:

> *some detergent*

Perfume is sold there.

Have some cheese.

They behave like count nouns when they refer to types or brands of a substance:

a strong detergent; some of the detergents on the market

a French perfume; men's perfumes

a tasty cheese; a range of cheeses

Collective nouns

Collective nouns refer to a group of people or things. These nouns can be used with either a plural or a singular verb, depending on whether you are thinking of something as a single entity, often an impersonal one, or as a number of individual people or things. If the noun is singular, it can be replaced by the pronoun *it*, and if it is plural, it can be replaced by the pronoun *they*. With the determiner *the*, or any of the possessive determiners like *my* or *your*, either a singular or a plural verb can be used:

Her family is wealthier than mine.

I'm still not sure if my family know where I am.

This government does not avoid making difficult decisions.

The government are to carry out a review of the situation.

The audience was asked to observe silence.

His audience always go absolutely wild at the end.

The British electorate believes in equality of opportunity.

Our electorate seem discouraged about the economy.

It seems that the press has become almost too powerful.

The press were invited in to take photos.

With a singular determiner, such as *a*, *an*, *another*, *this*, *that*, *which* or *no*, a singular verb is used:

An army is being recruited.

This crowd is nervous.

No jury is going to convict him.

The singular is usually used after words like *whole*, and the plural after words like *all* or *most*:

The whole crowd was shouting.

All my family were artists.

Some collective nouns have both singular and plural forms, like any count noun. The difference between them and normal count nouns is that even when they are used in the singular, their verb may be either singular or plural. Some common ones are *airforce*, *aristocracy*, *army*, *audience*, *band*, *cast*, *committee*, *company*, *crew*, *crowd*, *electorate*, *family*, *fire brigade*, *government*, *group*, *jury*, *middle class*, *navy*, *party*, *staff*, *team*, *tribe*, *troop*.

A few collective nouns only occur in the singular, that is, they are used with a determiner and have no plural form in particular senses. Although singular, they can still be used with a singular or plural verb. Some common ones are *artillery*, *citizenry*, *clientèle*, *defence*, *headquarters*, *majority*, *opposition*, *police*, *press*, *prosecution*, *public*.

A few are uncount. They can also be used with a singular or plural verb: *diamonds* etc (the four card suits), *graffiti*, *infantry*, *livestock*, *prey*, *trumps* (in cards).

Singular nouns

Some nouns are always singular in particular senses – they have no plural form. Examples include *abundance*, *aftermath*, *ambience*, *appreciation*, *brink*, *clamour*, *countdown*, *dark*, *exodus*, *forefront*, *gloom*, *horizon*, *mainland*, *maximum*, *outdoors*, *profusion*, *shame*, *throb*, *twinkle*, *waste* and *wealth*. They are like count nouns in that they are always used with a determiner like *a*, *an*, *the*, *my*, or *this*. They are used with a singular verb:

> *the* sun
>
> *the* moon
>
> *the* rain
>
> *my* past
>
> *a* strain
>
> *His* appearance *was dreadful.*
>
> *What a* fuss!
>
> *What a* din!
>
> *I was in a* hurry.
>
> *We had reached an* impasse.
>
> *Traffic was brought to a* standstill.
>
> *It was a* giggle.

Plural nouns

Some nouns are always plural in particular senses – they have no singular form. Examples include *alms*, *authorities*, *belongings*, *clothes*, *contents*, *dealings*, *dregs*, *earnings*, *fatigues*, *goods*, *groceries*, *lowlands*, *overalls*, *premises*, *proceedings*, *remains*, *surroundings*, *takings*, *thanks*, *travels* and *whereabouts*. If these nouns are used with a determiner, it is a plural determiner such as *some*, *these*, *those*, or *other*, or a determiner like *the* or *her* which can be used with either singular or plural forms. They are used with a plural verb:

these *scissors*

some *trousers*

his *spectacles*

warm *underclothes*

The *masses* elect their leader.

We kept *cattle*.

We want to get rid of the *vermin*.

He had *dreadlocks*.

The child was in *hysterics*.

Number

Number is the technical term used in grammar when asking if a noun is singular or plural. As pointed out above, plurals are usually formed by adding *-s* or *-es* to the singular. However, there are also many irregular plurals in English:

singular	plural
foot	feet
tooth	teeth
man	men
woman	women
child	children
goose	geese
sheep	sheep
louse	lice
mouse	mice
ox	oxen
penny	pence

NOUNS AND NOUN GROUPS

For the plural forms of individual nouns, you should consult a good dictionary.

Many nouns ending in *-s* are uncount and are therefore used with a singular verb. These nouns include diseases, eg *mumps*, *measles* and *rickets*, and games eg *billiards*, *bowls* and *skittles*. Nouns ending in *-ics*, used to refer to subjects of study and academic and other disciplines, eg *athletics*, *mathematics*, *genetics* and *forensics*, are also uncount and used with a singular verb.

Checklist

A **noun** is a naming word.

1. **Noun groups**
   - consists of a noun and can have more elements
   - the most important word is called the head

2. **General characteristics of nouns**
   - can be preceded by a determiner, a number or an adjective
   - can modify other nouns
   - can be followed by a prepositional phrase or a relative clause
   - can indicate possession

3. **Proper nouns**
   - name a person, place or thing that is unique
   - are usually written with an initial capital letter

4. **Common nouns**
   - do not name a particular person, place or thing
   - commonly have plural forms

5. Concrete nouns
- refer to something that can be touched or seen, eg *table*

6. Abstract nouns
- refer to qualities, ideas or experiences with no physical existence, eg *love*

7. Compound nouns
- consist of two or more words and can often be hyphenated

8. Count nouns
- refer to things that can be counted
- can have singular and plural forms

9. Uncount nouns
- refer to things that cannot be counted, such as substances, feelings, abstract concepts
- do not have plural forms

10. Mass nouns
- can behave like uncount nouns or count nouns, eg *some cheese*; *a hard cheese*

11. Collective nouns
- refer to a group of people or things, eg *family*
- can be used with a singular or plural verb

12. Singular nouns
- have no plural form and are used with a singular verb

13. Plural nouns
- are always plural in particular senses
- are used with a plural verb

14. Irregular plurals
- are not formed by adding *-s* or *-es* to the singular, eg *feet*

Grammar in practice

A Pick out the noun groups (including pronouns) in the following text:

> For this recipe you can use any winter vegetables that are available, for example cauliflower, carrots and onions. Start off by crushing the cumin, coriander and mustard seeds with a pestle and mortar. Then heat the oil in a medium saucepan and stir the prepared vegetables into it. Cook them over a fairly high heat until they're lightly browned, stirring frequently. Then turn the heat down low and stir in the crushed seeds, turmeric, cayenne, a seasoning of salt and pepper, and finally the yoghurt.

B Say whether the following nouns are count, uncount, both count and uncount, singular, plural or collective:

1 *answer*

2 *news*

3 *congratulations*

4 *sheep*

5 *education*

6 *coffee*

7 *mainland*

8 *grounding*

9 *committee*

10 *sunshine*

11 *decision*

12 *music*

13 *suicide*

14 *dreadlocks*

15 *cleanser*
16 *hurry*
17 *trousers*
18 *electorate*
19 *physics*
20 *livestock*

Verbs and phrasal verbs

Verbs are of two major types: the main verbs (also known as lexical verbs or full verbs) and the auxiliary verbs. They go together to form verb groups.

Main verbs

There are four types of main verb, corresponding to the major functions of the language we use. These are verbs that give information about:

- actions, eg *run*, *sew*, *walk*, *fall*, *jump*
- communication, eg *talk*, *argue*, *say*, *complain*
- mental processes and processes of perception, eg *think*, *believe*, *feel*, *see*
- states of being, eg *be*, *seem*, *exist*, *appear*

Regular verbs

Most verbs in English are regular verbs. In other words they have predictable endings in their different forms, which derive from the **base form** of the verb.

Main verbs have four forms:

- the **base form**, eg *jump*, *shout*, *walk*. The base form is, as its name implies, the form of the verb on which other forms are based. You use the base form for the **simple present tense**, except when it is in the third person singular (see below); the **imperative**, eg *stop*, *do enter*, *don't shout*; the **bare infinitive** eg *I saw him jump*, *I heard him shout*, *we must walk*; and finally the **to-infinitive**, eg *to jump*, *to shout*, *to walk*

- the **-s form**, which is the base form with an -s added. You use this form for the third person singular of the **simple present tense**, used with the pronouns *he*, *she* and *it*, or with singular nouns, eg *he jumps*, *she shouts*, *the door opens*

- the **-ing form**, which is the base form with -ing added, eg *jumping*, *shouting*, *walking*. This form has two uses. It is used as the **present participle**, eg *I like swimming*, *skiing is fun*. It is also used to form the **progressive tenses**, eg *she is watching*, *we were finishing*

- the **-ed form**, which is the base form with -ed added. This form has two uses. It is used for the **past tense**, eg *I jumped*, *she shouted*, *he walked*. Secondly, it is used for the **past participle**, eg *I have finished*, *she has stopped*, *we had objected*

Irregular verbs

Irregular verbs are those verbs in which the past tense and past participle are usually not formed by adding -ed to their base form. The past tense and past participle are often different from each other. These verbs may have three, four, or five different forms.

Irregular verbs can be grouped into five types:

- **type 1**
  verbs that have the same form for their base form, their past tense and their past participle. These verbs have only three different forms:

base form	-s form	-ing form	past tense	past participle
burst	bursts	bursting	burst	burst
cast	casts	casting	cast	cast
cost	costs	costing	cost	cost
cut	cuts	cutting	cut	cut

hit	hits	hitting	hit	hit
let	lets	letting	let	let
put	puts	putting	put	put
set	sets	setting	set	set
shut	shuts	shutting	shut	shut

- **type 2**

  verbs that have the same form for their base form and their past participle, but whose past tense is different. These verbs have four different forms:

base form	-s form	-ing form	past tense	past participle
become	becomes	becoming	became	become
come	comes	coming	came	come
run	runs	running	ran	run

- **type 3**

  verbs that have the same irregular forms for their past tense and their past participle. These verbs have four different forms:

base form	-s form	-ing form	past tense	past participle
bend	bends	bending	bent	bent
bind	binds	binding	bound	bound
bleed	bleeds	bleeding	bled	bled
bring	brings	bringing	brought	brought
build	builds	building	built	built
buy	buys	buying	bought	bought
catch	catches	catching	caught	caught
deal	deals	dealing	dealt	dealt
dig	digs	digging	dug	dug
feel	feels	feeling	felt	felt
fight	fights	fighting	fought	fought
find	finds	finding	found	found

get	gets	getting	got	got
have	has	having	had	had
hear	hears	hearing	heard	heard
hold	holds	holding	held	held
keep	keeps	keeping	kept	kept
lead	leads	leading	led	led
leave	leaves	leaving	left	left
make	makes	making	made	made
pay	pays	paying	paid	paid
say	says	saying	said	said
shoot	shoots	shooting	shot	shot
think	thinks	thinking	thought	thought

- **type 4**
  verbs that end in -*t* rather than -*ed*, in the past tense and the past participle but also have regular -*ed* forms. These verbs have four or five different forms:

base form	-*s* form	-*ing* form	past tense	past participle
burn	burns	burning	burnt/ burned	burnt/burned
dream	dreams	dreaming	dreamt/ dreamed	dreamt/ dreamed
kneel	kneels	kneeling	knelt/ kneeled	knelt/kneeled
learn	learns	learning	learnt/ learned	learnt/learned
light	lights	lighting	lit/lighted	lit/lighted
smell	smells	smelling	smelt/ smelled	smelt/smelled
spell	spells	spelling	spelt/spelled	spelt/spelled
spoil	spoils	spoiling	spoilt/ spoiled	spoilt/spoiled

- **type 5**

  verbs in which the base form, the past tense, and the past participle all have different forms. These verbs have five different forms:

base form	-s form	-ing form	past form	past participle
begin	begins	beginning	began	begun
bite	bites	biting	bit	bitten
break	breaks	breaking	broke	broken
choose	chooses	choosing	chose	chosen
draw	draws	drawing	drew	drawn
drink	drinks	drinking	drank	drunk
drive	drives	driving	drove	driven
eat	eats	eating	ate	eaten
fall	falls	falling	fell	fallen
fly	flies	flying	flew	flown
give	gives	giving	gave	given
go	goes	going	went	gone
grow	grows	growing	grew	grown
know	knows	knowing	knew	known
ring	rings	ringing	rang	rung
see	sees	seeing	saw	seen
sing	sings	singing	sang	sung
speak	speaks	speaking	spoke	spoken
swim	swims	swimming	swam	swum
take	takes	taking	took	taken
write	writes	writing	wrote	written

Spelling

Note that there are some regular rules for spelling the various forms of main verbs. Rules for the base form and the **-s form** apply to regular and irregular verbs, while rules for the **-ed form** apply only to regular verbs.

- For verbs that end in *o*, *ch*, *sh*, *ss*, *x*, *z* and *zz* in their base form, you form the **-s form** by adding *-es* rather than *-s*, eg *matches*, *rushes*, *hisses*, *taxes*, *buzzes*. Where the base form of a verb ends in a consonant followed by *y*, the third person singular present is formed by changing the *y* to *i* and adding *-es*, eg *buries*, *flies*, *dries*, *marries*, *tries*, *worries*, *accompanies*. Where the base form ends in a vowel followed by *y*, the form does not change to *-ies*, eg *says*, *enjoys*, *buys*.

- The **-ing form**: if the base form ends in a consonant plus *e*, the *e* is dropped before adding *-ing*, eg *living*, *making*, *dating*, *hoping*. When the base form ends in *ie*, the *i* becomes *y* and the *e* is dropped when adding *-ing*, eg *dying*, *lying*. If the base form ends in *ye*, *ee* or *oe*, the final *e* is not dropped when adding the *-ing*, eg: *dyeing*, *fleeing*, *shoeing*. Verbs that end in a short vowel and then a consonant double the final consonant in the *-ing* form, eg *tapping*, *dripping*, *grinning*, *bobbing*, *permitting*, *stopping*, *running*. If the base form ends in *c*, the ending becomes *ck* when the *-ing* is added, eg *mimicking*, *frolicking*.

- The **-ed form**: when the base form ends in *e*, only *d* is added, eg *died*, *pursued*, *agreed*, *received*. If the base form ends in *c*, the ending becomes *ck* in the *-ed* form, eg *mimicked*, *frolicked*. Verbs that end in a consonant also double this consonant in the *-ed* form, eg *tapped*, *dripped*, *grinned*, *bobbed*, *permitted*, *stopped*.

Transitive and intransitive verbs

Main verbs in English may be either transitive or intransitive, or both.

Transitive verbs

These are used with a **direct object**. Most verbs, that is, those referring to actions, communication etc, are used with a direct object:

She examined it closely.

The other car hit him head on.

The mountains reminded me of home.

A new postman delivered our mail this morning.

The direct objects in the above examples are *it*, *him*, *me*, *our mail*. Main verbs that are always transitive include *afford*, *allow*, *bring*, *deny*, *enjoy*, *excuse*, *fix*, *get*, *have*, *let*, *like*, *make*, *mean*, *need*, *owe*, *prefer*, *prove*, *put*, *rob*, *wrap*. There are many thousands of these, and a good dictionary will have entries for all of them.

Some verbs are **ditransitive**; that is, they may have two objects: a direct object and an **indirect object**:

I bought her chocolates.

She gave me a kiss.

They paid John a million pounds.

He told her he was not going to leave them anything in his will.

Her, *me*, *John* and *them* in the above examples are indirect objects. *Chocolates*, *a kiss*, *a million pounds* and *anything* are all direct objects.

Some verbs are used with a direct object and an **object complement**:

He named his son Sebastian.

They appointed her editor of the newspaper.

We considered him a dangerous man.

Sebastian, *editor of the newspaper* and *a dangerous man* are all object complements.

Most transitive verbs can be used in **passive** verb groups (see pages 66–8). All the examples we give here are of **active** verb groups.

Intransitive verbs

These are verbs that are not used with an object; they can be used with nothing after them at all:

> *When I asked her about it, she lied.*
>
> *Emily sneezed loudly.*
>
> *She has just arrived.*
>
> *I shook hands with him and left.*

Verbs that are always intransitive include *break down*, *come*, *compete*, *digress*, *disappear*, *fall*, *get out*, *get up*, *queue*, *rise*, *turn up*. Intransitive verbs cannot be used in passive verb groups.

Transitive and intransitive verbs

Many verbs are both transitive and intransitive, that is, they can be used with or without an object:

> *I invited her and she accepted.*
>
> *He offered his help, and I accepted the offer.*
>
> *John and Judy decided to adopt.*
>
> *They adopted a child.*
>
> *Have you finished?*
>
> *I'm just finishing my meal.*

Verbs that can be transitive or intransitive include *answer*, *attack*, *cook*, *defend*, *drink*, *drive*, *eat*, *explain*, *fly*, *hear*, *kill*, *remember*, *speak*, *travel*, *watch*.

Link verbs

Link verbs are verbs that are used to talk about states of being, becoming, seeming etc. They are different from transitive verbs in that they are followed by a **complement** rather than an object. The complement may be either a noun group or an adjective group. By far the most common is the verb *be*:

> *My wife is a doctor.*
>
> *I am rather tired.*

Other common link verbs are *appear*, *become*, *comprise*, *equal*, *feel*, *form*, *go*, *grow*, *look*, *remain*, *represent*, *seem*, *smell*, *sound*, *taste*, *turn*. Many of these, like *go* and *grow*, are link verbs in only one of their senses. Here are some examples:

> *I have become very interested in Islam.*
>
> *Twelve minus three equals nine.*
>
> *I felt such a fool.*
>
> *He went red in the face.*
>
> *You don't look very well.*
>
> *That sounds a good idea.*

Very interested in Islam, *nine*, *such a fool*, *red in the face*, *very well* and *a good idea* are all complements.

Ergative verbs

An ergative verb can be used either transitively to focus on the person who performs an action or intransitively to focus on the thing affected by an action:

She broke the window.

The window broke.

We sailed the boat up the river.

The boat sailed up the river.

Dissolve the sugar in warm water.

Sugar dissolves in warm water.

Note that these verbs are different from the transitive/intransitive verbs like *drive* or *eat*. With the latter, the subject stays the same whether or not there is an object, eg *I drank*, *I drank some water*. With ergative verbs, the subject changes according to whether the verb is being used transitively or intransitively.

Reciprocal verbs

Reciprocal verbs describe actions in which two or more people or groups do the same thing to each other. They are used in two ways. First, they can be used with a plural subject to show that people or groups are interacting. Second, they can be used with a singular subject which refers to one participant and introduces the other participant using the preposition *with*:

We quarrelled.

I quarrelled with her.

Britain and Germany have reached a compromise.

Britain has reached a compromise with Germany.

Auxiliary verbs

Auxiliary verbs are sometimes known as 'helping verbs'. They combine with main verbs to form verb groups indicating tense and aspect. There are three auxiliaries: *be*, *do* and *have*. The verb *get* is also sometimes used as an auxiliary.

Be

The verb *be* is an irregular verb with a greater number of forms than any other verbs (eight forms):

> *be* (base form)
>
> *am*, *is*, *are* (simple present tense)
>
> *was*, *were* (simple past tense)
>
> *being* (*-ing* form, or present participle)
>
> *been* (past participle)

Be is used as an auxiliary in the following ways:

- to form the **progressive tenses** (see pages 57–9). These are formed from *be* plus the *-ing* form (the present participle) of a main verb:

> *I am listening.*
>
> *We were eating.*

- to form **passive verb groups**. (See the section on active and passive verb groups on pages 66–8.) These are formed from *be* plus the *-ed* form (the past participle) of the main verb:

> *She was killed.*
>
> *All the cakes had been eaten.*

- to form **tag questions** (see page 70):

> *She isn't laughing, is she?*
>
> *I am hurrying, aren't I?*

Be has the following **contractions** or shortened forms, which are used in speech and informal situations: *I'm*, *you're*, *he's*, *she's*, *it's*, *we're*, *they're*. When the verb group is negative, the following choices are available: *I'm not* (note that we cannot say *I amn't*), *you're not* or *you aren't*, *he's not* or *he isn't*, *we're not* or *we aren't*, *they're not* or *they aren't*. The simple past forms are *I wasn't*, *we weren't* etc. The forms used in negative questions and tag questions are *aren't I? isn't he? weren't we?* etc.

Note that *be* is also a main or a lexical verb, with all the normal tenses, eg *You're being silly*, *She was overweight*, *I have been a builder*.

Do

The verb *do* is an irregular verb with the following forms:

> *do* (base form)
>
> *do, does* (simple present tense)
>
> *did* (simple past tense)
>
> *doing* (-ing form, or present participle)
>
> *done* (past participle)

Do is used as an auxiliary in the following ways (note that only the simple present and simple past tenses of *do* are used):

- to form **questions** when the tense is simple present or simple past:

> *Do you want to leave?*
>
> *Does he play the guitar?*
>
> *Did you see the film?*

- to form **negatives** when the tense is simple present or simple past:

> *She doesn't like him.*
>
> *I don't want to eat now.*
>
> *I didn't say anything.*

The indicative and positive forms of these questions and negatives does not contain *do*: *I want to leave*, *She likes him* etc.

- to form **tag questions**:

> *You enjoyed the party, didn't you?*
>
> *We didn't have much fun, did we?*

- to emphasize the main verb:

> *I do like you.*
>
> *I did write to you.*
>
> *Do come in.*

Do has the following contractions, which are used in speech and informal situations: *I don't*, *he doesn't*, *we didn't* etc. In negative questions and tag questions, the forms are *don't I?*, *didn't he?* etc.

Note that *do* is also a main or lexical verb, with all the normal tenses, eg *I'm doing my homework*, *He did it!*

Have

The verb *have* is an irregular verb with the following forms:

> *have (base form)*
>
> *have, has (simple present tense)*

having (-ing form, or present participle)

had (simple past tense and past participle)

Have is used as an auxiliary in the following ways:

- to form the **compound tenses**. These are formed from *have* plus the *-ed* form (the past participle) of the main verb:

    I have succeeded.
    They had finished.

- to form **tag questions** when you are using a perfect tense:

    He has arrived, hasn't he?
    We haven't met, have we?
    She had succeeded at last, hadn't she?

Have also has contractions, which are used in speech and informal situations: *I've, you've, he's, she's, it's, we've, they've.* In negative questions and question tags, there are the following choices: *I haven't* or *I've not, I hadn't* or *I'd not* etc.

Note that *have* is also a main or lexical verb, with all the normal tenses, eg *You have a lovely house, I had such a shock.*

Get

The verb *get* is also used as an auxiliary in the following two ways:

- to form **passive verb groups**:

    She got knocked down by a car.

● to indicate that an action, especially something difficult, has been achieved:

   I finally got started.

Modals

Modal auxiliaries

The modal auxiliaries (also known as **modal verbs**, **modal operators**, or simply **modals**) are *can*, *could*, *may*, *might*, *should*, *would*, *must*, *shall*, *will*. Modal auxiliaries can be distinguished from the other auxiliaries because they have only one form (the base form). They are never preceded by *to*. Modals combine with main verbs to form verb groups.

Modals are used in statements expressing ability, possibility, permission, necessity and obligation, degrees of likelihood or probability, and prediction.

   You must know what I mean.

   Joan should arrive soon.

   Maybe you can understand my position.

   I would help you, only I'm busy.

They can also be used in **questions** or to form **tag questions**:

   May I ask what you are doing here?

   Must you leave?

   You'll look after me, won't you?

   He can't help worrying, can he?

Will and *shall* are often contracted to *'ll*. When negative, modals also have contractions: *can't*, *couldn't*, *mightn't* etc. (*Mayn't* is rare.) The negative contractions of *will* and *shall* are *won't* and *shan't*.

Semi-modals

The semi-modals are the verbs *dare* and *need*. They sometimes behave like modals, eg *I didn't dare tell my uncle*, and sometimes like ordinary verbs, eg *We don't dare to raise our interest rates*.

Phrasal modals

Phrasal modals have a lot in common with modals, but they are phrases of two or more words. Some of them are: *be able to*, *be bound to*, *be going to*, *be liable to*, *be supposed to*, *ought to*, *used to*, *would rather*. When they begin with *be*, the form changes depending on the subject and the tense, eg *I am bound to pass*, *He was bound to pass*, but when they do not begin with *be* their form does not change, eg *I would rather walk*, *He would rather walk*.

Phrasal verbs

A phrasal verb is a verb followed by an adverb or a preposition. It may also be followed by an adverb and then a preposition. The combination of the verb with the adverb and/or preposition makes a new verb with a new meaning, often one that is idiomatic. The adverbs and prepositions used in phrasal verbs are known as **particles**.

Here are some examples:

> *I had to* look after *the baby all day.*
> *I need a few days' peace so that I can* wind down.
> *Have a think and see what you can* come up with.
> *He'll do anything if he feels he can* get away with *it.*
> *I'm* looking forward to *my holiday.*

Like normal verbs, some phrasal verbs are transitive and are used with an object; others are intransitive and are not used with an object, and some are both transitive and intransitive.

When a phrasal verb is transitive, and the particle is an adverb, the object may follow the particle or it may come between the verb and the particle. If the object is a pronoun, it must come between the verb and the particle:

> *Look up the difficult words in a dictionary.*
>
> *Look it up in a dictionary.*
>
> *Ring up the police straightaway.*
>
> *Ring me up tonight.*
>
> *Dad'll freak out if he finds you here.*
>
> *This news will probably freak him out.*

Checklist

There are two types of **verbs**: main and auxiliary.

1. **Main verbs**
   * give information about actions, communications, mental processes and states of being.

2. **Regular verbs**
   * have predictable endings derived from the base form of the verb

3. **Irregular verbs**
   * have variable endings, eg *run/ran*
   * have a different past tense and past participle

4. **Transitive verbs**
   * are used with a direct object, eg *The car hit <u>him</u>*

5. Ditransitive verbs
- can have two objects: direct and indirect, eg *I bought her chocolates*
- can have a direct object and an object complement, eg *He named his son Sebastian*

6. Intransitive verbs
- are not used with an object, eg *He lied*

7. Link verbs
- are used to talk about states of becoming, being etc
- are followed by a complement rather than an object, eg *He appears very sad*

8. Ergative verbs
- can be used to focus either on the subject on the object of the action, eg *She rang the bell*; *The bell rang*

9. Reciprocal verbs
- describe actions in which people do the same thing to each other, eg *We quarrelled*

10. Auxiliary verbs
- combine with main verbs to indicate tense and aspect
- are *be*, *do*, *have* and *get*

11. Modal auxiliaries
- have only one form (base form) and are never preceded by *to*
- are *can*, *could*, *may*, *might*, *should*, *would*, *must*, *shall*, *will*

12. Semi-modals
- are the verbs *dare* and *need*
- sometimes behave as modals and sometimes like ordinary verbs

13. Phrasal modals
- are similar to modals but are phrases of two or more words, eg *be liable to*

14. Phrasal verbs
- are verbs followed by a particle, which is an adverb and/or a preposition, eg *look after*
- can be transitive, intransitive or both

Grammar in practice

A Say whether the following verbs are transitive, intransitive, both transitive and intransitive, link, ergative or reciprocal:

1 *ask*

2 *pay*

3 *melt*

4 *fight*

5 *become*

6 *disappear*

7 *kill*

8 *control*

9 *attack*

10 *dance*

11 *laugh*

12 *change*

13 *drive*

14 *reverse*

15 *hear*

16 *handle*

17 *throw*

18 *disagree*

19 *matter*

20 *remove*

B Make a list of five phrasal verbs using the following verbs and a particle:

1 *give*

2 *look*

3 *break*

4 *write*

5 *talk*

Verb tenses

A verb tense is a particular form or set of forms of a verb that show at what time the action or the process of the verb takes place. There are only two basic tense forms in English in the sense that there are only two different ways that a verb changes to indicate time. These tenses are the **simple present** (eg *talk/talks*, *go/goes*, *come/comes*, *am/is/are*, *have/has*, *run/runs*) and the **simple past** (eg *talked*, *went*, *came*, *was/were*, *had*, *ran*).

In many other languages, by contrast, there may be many forms of a particular verb, each used to refer to present, past, or future time, as anyone who has studied Latin will know.

Even though there may be, strictly speaking, only two main English tenses, various combinations of these two tenses with forms of the auxiliary verbs *be* and *have* can also be broadly defined as tenses. These combinations are known as **compound tenses**. They are described later in this chapter.

In use, both simple and compound tenses form verb groups, whether they consist of one or of several words eg *Mary went* (simple) or *Mary has gone* (compound). It may seem odd to call a single main verb a group, but the reason for this is that it fulfils the same function in a sentence as a compound tense consisting of more than one word.

(Note that the examples below are all in the **active voice**, to make it easier to see the differences between the tenses. The formation of the **passive** is dealt with on pages 66–8.)

Simple tenses

Simple present tense

The table below shows the forms of the simple present tense using the verb *move*:

singular	plural
I *move*	we *move*
you *move*	you *move*
he/she/it *moves*	they *move*

The simple present tense uses the base form of the verb, which changes only in the third person singular, eg *I go*, *she goes*. Questions, tag questions and negatives are formed using *do* and *does*.

The uses of the simple present tense are:

- to state timeless truths or facts:

    The moon orbits the Earth.

    Hot air rises.

    Does it snow in Algeria?

    It doesn't often rain in August.

- to make statements about habitual actions:

    I catch the bus at 7.30 am.

    My son phones me every Sunday.

    Do you go to school?

    I don't work on Tuesdays.

VERB TENSES

- to make statements about permanent or unchanging actions or situations:

  He farms 300 acres.

  She drinks a lot.

  Do you take sugar in your tea?

  He doesn't eat much.

- to express opinions, attitudes, observations and declarations:

  Harriet hates hanging about waiting.

  She says she hasn't heard from Henry for six months.

  I see they've sold their flat.

  'They've sold their house.' 'So I gather.'

  I swear I saw a mouse in the kitchen.

  I hope you're wrong.

  Do you like my new tie?

- to refer to scheduled events:

  Our plane leaves at six in the morning

  The film festival starts next week.

  What time does the store open?

- to give a sense of immediacy, for example in sports commentaries:

  He shoots. Yes, he scores. A brilliant goal!

- to talk about the past in a dramatic way, for example in novels and jokes:

  She goes into this shop and asks for a pound of lean mince. Turns out it's an ironmonger's, not a butcher's.

The thief jumps into a getaway car, which speeds off.

- to write newspaper headlines or headlines on the radio or television that refer to events in the very recent past:

    Farmers march through London

    Beckham weds

    American wins Wimbledon

Simple past tense

The table below shows the forms of the simple past tense using the verb *arrive*:

singular	**plural**
I *arrived*	we *arrived*
you *arrived*	you *arrived*
he/she/it *arrived*	they *arrived*

The simple past tense uses the past tense form of the verb, eg *went*, *spoke*, *believed*. Questions, question tags and negatives are formed using *did*.

The uses of the simple past tense are:

- to refer to particular actions that were done or completed in the past:

    They mowed the lawn and tidied the borders.

    He moved to Australia last year.

    Jane broke her ankle playing hockey.

    Did you see that?

    I didn't go to the party.

- to refer to a state that existed in the past:

    Arthur seemed upset.

    Georgina was once in the police force.

- to refer to actions or events that occurred as a matter of habit or routine in the past:

    He never played football as a boy.

    They always had roast beef on Sundays.

    Did you go sailing when you were young?

- to make polite or tentative requests or suggestions:

    I just thought you might need a break.

    Did you want to take out insurance on your fridge?

- to report indirect speech:

    He complained that he was broke.

    Did you say you wanted to apply?

- to express something that is hypothetical, especially in an *if* clause:

    If you ate less, you'd be healthier.

    I wish I had more time.

Compound tenses

Compound tenses show **aspect** rather than actual time reference. Aspect shows how an action or event is to be regarded with respect to time, rather than its actual location in time. There are two kinds of aspect, **perfect** and **progressive** (or **continuous**). The perfect aspect is used to show that an action or event has continued up to the present, is complete at the time of speaking or was complete at the time being referred to. The progressive aspect is used to show that an action or event is in progress or is incomplete at the time of speaking.

There are six compound tenses.

Present perfect

The present perfect is formed from the present tense of the auxiliary verb *have* plus the *-ed* form (the past participle) of a main verb. It is used to relate a situation or action to the present:

> He *has gone* home.
>
> I *have* already *eaten.*
>
> Susie *has finished* her work.
>
> *Have* you *seen* John?
>
> I *haven't been* to New York.

Past perfect

The past perfect is formed from the past tense of the auxiliary verb *have* plus the *-ed* form (the past participle) of a main verb. It is used to relate a completed situation or action to some time in the past:

> He *had gone* home by the time I got round to ringing the office.
>
> I felt ill. I *had eaten* far too much.
>
> She *hadn't finished* her breakfast.
>
> *Had* you already *left* when she arrived?

Present progressive

The present progressive (or continuous) is formed from the present tense of the auxiliary verb *be* plus the *-ing* form (the present participle) of the main verb. It is used to refer to something that is in progress at the time of speaking, to a present state or to a habitual action:

> Look Mum, I'm hanging upside down.
>
> What are you doing? I'm planting daffodils.
>
> Is your cold getting any better?
>
> I'm living in London at the moment.
>
> He's always making mistakes like that.

Past progressive

The past progressive (or continuous) is formed from the past tense of the auxiliary verb be plus the -ing form (the present participle) of the main verb. It is used to refer to something that was in progress at some time in the past, or to a past state:

> Inflation was rising at the time.
>
> I was chopping garlic when I cut my thumb.
>
> We believed in what we were doing.
>
> Where were you working?
>
> He was living in France.

Present perfect progressive

The present perfect progressive (or continuous) is formed from the present tense of the auxiliary verb have plus been and then the -ing form (the present participle) of a main verb. It is used to refer to actions or situations that began in the past and are still continuing in the present:

> I have been working round the clock for days.
>
> We've been sitting here for more than two hours.
>
> I've been collecting shells since I was a child.
>
> How long have you been working there?

Past perfect progressive

The past perfect progressive (or continuous) is formed from the past tense of the auxiliary verb *have* plus *been* and then the *-ing* form (the present participle) of a main verb. It is used to refer to actions or situations that began in the past and were already completed before the point in the past being referred to:

> *I had been working round the clock for days.*

> *By the time he arrived, we had been waiting for two hours.*

Future time

There are several ways in which future time is indicated in English:

- You can use the modal auxiliaries *will* or *shall* plus the base form of a main verb. *Shall* is only used with the pronouns *I* or *we*:

> *What I shall do is put some filler in the cracks.*

> *She will ring you tonight.*

> *I'll give him your message when I see him.*

> *They've gone and they won't come here again.*

> *We'll arrive about four o'clock your time.*

> *Future generations will wonder how we could live in such a polluted atmosphere.*

> *I shan't use that shampoo again. It brought me out in a rash.*

- You can use the phrasal modal *be going to* plus the base form of a main verb. This is used especially when something has been decided and the intention is to carry it out, or when predicting what will happen:

At the moment he says he's going to study architecture, but he might change his mind.

We are going to make some pretty radical changes in the very near future.

They're going to have a party.

You're going to get ill if you don't eat properly.

- As mentioned above, you can use the present progressive tense to refer to scheduled events:

  We're getting a new carpet tomorrow.

  He's making a big speech on Friday.

  Are you having your baby at home or in hospital?

- As mentioned above, you can use the simple present tense with a future meaning to refer to scheduled events:

  Kirsty moves into her new flat in December.

  Hurry up. Our plane leaves in 20 minutes.

- You can use the **future progressive**, which is formed with the modal auxiliaries *will* or *shall* plus the auxiliary verb *be* and then the *-ing* form (the present participle) of a main verb. You use this to refer to something that will or is likely to happen at some indefinite time in the future:

  I'll be moving into my new flat sometime soon.

  He'll be telling me how to do my job next, I expect.

- You can use the **future perfect**, which is formed from the auxiliary verbs *will* or *shall* and *have* plus the *-ed* form (the past participle) of a main verb to talk about actions that will be completed at a time in the future before something else happens:

Let's have a party next week. We shall have finished the decorating by then.

She will have prepared a big meal as usual.

- You can also use the auxiliary verb *be* plus a *to*-infinitive when you refer to something that has been arranged or planned. This is a formal use.

   He is to appear at the Crown Court on 5 April.

   You are to tell him that this is the last time I shall warn him.

- You can use a **phrasal modal**, such as *be about to* plus the base form of a main verb, or *be on the point of* plus the *-ing* form of a main verb, to say that something will happen very soon. You can use *be due to* plus the base form of a main verb, when something is intended to happen, or you can use *be bound to* plus the base form of a main verb when something is sure to happen:

   I'm about to leave now.

   He's on the point of resigning.

   The bus is due to depart at nine.

   Don't worry. He's bound to phone soon.

Checklist

In English there are two simple tenses and six compound tenses that show at what time the action or process of a **verb** takes place.

1. **Simple present tense is used:**
   - to state timeless facts or make statements about habitual actions or unchanging situations
   - to talk about the past in a dramatic way
   - to refer to scheduled events

2. **Simple past tense is used:**
   - to refer to actions done or completed in the past
   - to refer to actions or events that occurred habitually in the past
   - to make polite requests or suggestions or express something hypothetical
   - to report indirect speech

3. **Compound tenses**
   - can show perfect aspect (an action that has continued to the present) or progressive (to show an action that is still in progress or incomplete)

4. **Present perfect**
   - present tense of the auxiliary verb *have* plus the past participle of the main verb
   - is used to relate a situation or action to the present, eg *He has gone home*

5. **Past perfect**
   - past tense of the auxiliary verb *have* plus the past participle of the main verb
   - is used to relate a completed action to some time in the past, eg *I had finished by this morning*

6. Present progressive

- present tense of the auxiliary verb *be* plus the present participle of the main verb
- is used to refer to something that is in progress at the time of speaking or to a habitual action, eg *I'm singing the lead in a West End musical*

7. Past progressive (past continuous)

- past tense of the auxiliary verb *be* plus the present participle of the main verb
- is used to refer to something that was in progress at some time in the past, or to a past state, eg *I was working in Chicago then*

8. Present perfect progressive (present perfect continuous)

- present tense of the auxiliary verb *have* plus *been* and then the present participle of a main verb
- is used to refer to actions or situations that began in the past and are still continuing in the present, eg *I have been waiting here for hours*

9. Perfect progressive (perfect continuous)

- past tense of the auxiliary verb *have* plus *been* and then the present participle of a main verb
- is used to refer to actions or situations that began in the past and were already completed before the point in the past being referred to, eg *I had been waiting there for hours by the time they arrived*

10. Future time can be indicated by:

- using modal auxiliaries *will* or *shall* plus the base form of the verb eg *I shall ring her when I get home*
- using the phrasal modal *be going* plus the base form of the verb, eg *I'm going to throw a party*

- using the present progressive tense (to refer to scheduled events), eg *He's arriving tomorrow*
- using the simple present tense, eg *The shop closes in ten minutes*
- using the future progressive, eg *He'll be arriving soon*
- using the future perfect, eg *I'll have cooked dinner by the time he arrives*
- using the auxiliary verb *be* plus the infinitive to refer to something planned, eg *Everyone is to be in their seats by 7.30 sharp*
- using a phrasal modal to say something will happen soon, eg *It's about to rain*

Grammar in practice

A Name the tense of the following sentences:

1 *The thieves stole my credit card.*

2 *I've been waiting ages for you.*

3 *I'll have finished everything by lunch time.*

4 *We will be fighting a losing battle for our land.*

5 *I have complied with all your requests.*

6 *I don't want to talk about it.*

7 *He had been working fifteen-hour days.*

8 *They're sitting on the lawn having tea.*

9 *Mr Jones had signed nothing yet.*

10 *I was listening to him carefully.*

B Pick out the auxiliary and modal auxiliary verbs in the following sentences:

1 *The troops should pull out of the country immediately.*

2 *Your home life may suffer if you have problems at work.*

3 *Now that the children have grown up, we can do our own thing.*

4 *Dawn was approaching as we left the house.*

5 *'What's going on here?' he demanded.*

6 *John looked at her, but she didn't notice.*

7 *I would tell you if I knew, but I don't.*

8 *She must have been about my age.*

9 *From where I sat, I could see a palm tree.*

10 *I was thinking that I might move in for a while.*

More about verb groups

In previous chapters we talked about types of verb and verb tense. This chapter is about the verb group, which functions as the **predicate** (see pages 7–8) in a clause or sentence. A verb group may consist of one or more words. The main verb is the nucleus of the group, and is often called the **head**.

Active and passive verb groups

So far all the examples of tenses that we have given were active verb groups. But in English, transitive verbs that are used with an object can be active or passive. This is known as **voice**.

A verb group in the **active voice** is one whose subject performs the action of the verb. The subject comes before the verb group, and the object comes after it, in sentences like *Elephants destroyed their entire crop*. A verb group in the **passive voice** is one whose subject is the person or thing that the action is done to, so it comes at the beginning of the clause, as in *Their entire crop was destroyed by elephants*. Most transitive and ditransitive verbs can be used in the passive.

The passive is formed by the auxiliary verb *be* plus the *-ed* form (the past participle) of a main verb. So if the tense is simple present for example, you use the simple past form of the verb *be*, and then the past participle. If the tense is present or past perfect, you use *have/has/had been* before the past participle:

> *The museum is funded by the City Council.*
> [simple present]

He was attacked by muggers.
[simple past]

A lot of mistakes are being made.
[present progressive]

The method of electing the president was being changed.
[past progressive]

He has been struck by lightning.
[present perfect]

She had been accepted by the whole group.
[past perfect]

The meeting will be held at nine o'clock.
[future time]

The photocopier is going to be replaced.
[future time]

The decorating will have been finished by then.
[future perfect]

With modals, you use the modal plus *be* and then the past participle of the main verb:

> *It can't be helped.*

> *You will be expected to participate in team games.*

The present perfect progressive and the past perfect progressive are not often used in the passive. For example, you would not say *She has been being exploited at work*. You would use an active verb group, as in *They have been exploiting her at work*.

Some passive verb groups are followed by an adjunct beginning with *by* as in some of the examples above. But in fact the vast majority of passives are not followed by *by*. This is because we choose the passive for a reason: we may not know or may not want to say who or what is responsible for an action. Or it may just be that it is unimportant:

> Breakfast *is served*.
>
> A room *has been reserved* for you.
>
> The name of the winner *will be announced* tomorrow.
>
> A lot of research into climate change *is* now *being done*.

> **Usage**
>
> The passive is far less common than the active. It has been calculated that passives make up only ten percent of what we write or say. Many style guides advise against over-using the passive, because the active is simpler and more direct.

In conversation, *get* is often used instead of *be* to form the passive:

> He *got arrested* for burglary.
>
> My hair *gets cut* monthly.

> **Usage**
>
> Many people regard this usage as too informal. It is better to avoid it in formal contexts.

Finite and non-finite verb groups

A verb group in its finite form has tense and aspect:

> I *go* to school every day.
>
> I *went* to school every day.
>
> She *has eaten* a big meal.

It also shows number and person (although only the third person singular has a particular ending for person, apart from the verb *be*, which has different forms for *I*, *you*, and *he/she/it*):

She writes detective stories.

They write to each other regularly.

Some verb groups are **non-finite**. Non-finite verb groups do not show tense, aspect, number or person. The subject does not determine their form. The non-finite forms are the *to*-infinitive, the *-ing* form and the *-ed* form (the past participle):

She'll need a bit of time to recover from the operation.

Riding bareback can be pretty uncomfortable.

He'll only resign if forced to do so.

See pages 175–6 for more information on finite and non-finite verbs and clauses.

The mood of verb groups

Verb groups can have any one of four moods: **indicative**, **interrogative**, **imperative** and **subjunctive**.

Indicative mood

The indicative mood is used for making statements, which may be positive or negative:

He went home.

Connie loves flowers.

He's busy.

Hannah isn't listening.

I haven't seen anyone.

Interrogative mood

The interrogative mood is used for asking questions. There are two types of question. The first type is a question for which the answer is either 'yes' or 'no'; this type is known as a **yes/no question** or a **polar question**. Yes/no questions are formed from the auxiliaries *do* or *have*, or a modal auxiliary like *should* or *can*:

> *Do you want a piece of advice?*
>
> *Have you got your keys?*
>
> *Can you hear that noise?*

The second type of question begins with one of the interrogative determiners *which*, *what* or *whose*; with one of the interrogative pronouns *who*, *whom*, *whose*, *which* or *what*; or an adverb like *how*, *when* or *where*. These questions anticipate a fuller answer than yes/no questions:

> *What time is it?*
>
> *Whose bag is this?*
>
> *Who does she want to see?*
>
> *Which chair are you going to sit in?*
>
> *How are you?*
>
> *When did you see him last?*

In conversation, people often end a sentence with a short phrase in the form of a question. These interrogative phrases are known as **tag questions**. They may be positive or negative, and are used to elicit a confirmation of a statement. Generally, a positive statement is followed by a negative question tag, and a negative statement is followed by a positive tag question:

> *They were booked on this flight, weren't they?*
>
> *You're Spanish, aren't you?*
>
> *It isn't Friday already, is it?*
>
> *You didn't say that to her, did you?*

Occasionally a positive tag is used with a positive statement to express surprise, disbelief, anger, sarcasm etc:

So you're a bit of a chef, are you?

Imperative mood

The imperative mood is used when giving orders, commands and instructions. An imperative verb group usually has no subject before it. The basic structure is a verb group followed by an object. You can use *do* at the beginning of the verb group to emphasize an imperative:

Go home!

Get down from that wall at once!

Hurry, children.

Grip the cork firmly, and pull it carefully upwards.

Do help yourself.

Negative imperative verb groups begin with the auxiliary *do* followed by *not*, or by the contracted form *don't*:

Don't worry.

Don't look at me like that.

Don't make such a noise.

Occasionally an imperative main group has *you* as a subject. It is used to make an order more forceful:

You just listen to me!

Subjunctive mood

The subjunctive mood is used for talking about wishes and hypothetical or unreal situations. Note that you use *were* instead of *was*:

I wish it were all over.

If that were the case, he would have been arrested by now.

If I were you, I'd get rid of it.

The subjunctive is also used to talk about requests, proposals, demands etc. The base form of the verb is used rather than the third person *-s* form. It is only the third person singular that is affected:

I faxed him asking that he send the report directly to head office.

I suggested that he remain silent on the matter.

It is not required that she retire at sixty.

She requests that the family be left alone to mourn.

There are also some fixed phrases where the verb group is subjunctive:

Heaven forbid!

God bless you.

Come what may ...

Suffice it to say ...

Note that the subjunctive mood is being used less and less. Many people use phrases such as, *If that was the case ...*

Checklist

A **verb group** may consist of one or more words. The main verb is the nucleus of the group, and is often called the head.

1. A verb group in the active voice

- is one whose subject performs the action of the verb, eg *Elephants destroyed their crop*

2. A verb group in the passive voice

- is one whose subject is the person or thing that the action is done to, eg *Their entire crop was destroyed by elephants*
- is formed by the auxiliary verb *be* plus the past participle of a main verb, eg *Land was sighted at daybreak*
- can also be formed by using the modal plus *be* and the past participle, eg *Full attendance will be expected*
- is often formed by the verb *get* in informal speech, eg *The burglar got caught red-handed*

3. Finite verb groups

- have tense and aspect, eg *He drives to work every day*

4. Non-finite verb groups

- do not show tense, aspect or number, eg *Sailing can be fun*
- are the infinitive, the present participle and the past participle

5. Indicative mood

- is used for making statements, eg *France won the match*

6. Interrogative mood

- is used for asking questions

7. Imperative mood

- is used when giving orders, commands and instructions

8. **Negative imperative mood**
- is formed with the auxiliary *do* followed by *not*, or by the contracted form *don't*, eg *Don't forget to ring me!*

9. **Subjunctive mood**
- is used for talking about wishes and hypothetical or unreal situations, eg *If only I <u>were</u> on a beach now*
- is also used to talk about requests, proposals and demands, eg *The authorities demand that he <u>give</u> himself up now*
- is also used in fixed phrases, eg *God <u>save</u> the Queen*

Grammar in practice

A Underline the passive verb groups in the following sentences:

1 *The company's goals have never been achieved.*
2 *The game cannot be cancelled at this late stage.*
3 *The painting is owned by a private collector.*
4 *Mo was actually christened Julianne.*
5 *A few months in a monastery has been suggested.*

B Put the verb in brackets in an appropriate passive form:

1 *Last year she .... as suffering from autism. (diagnose)*
2 *The festival .... successfully for the last few years. (run)*
3 *We are hoping that the bill .... next autumn. (pass)*

    4 *Little ....about what happened to ordinary people during the Revolution. (write)*

    5 *By the time we arrived, the building .... to the ground. (burn)*

C State the mood of the following sentences:

    1 *Most of the buildings have been torn down.*

    2 *Who do you know in the armed forces?*

    3 *Go away!*

    4 *The police requested that the building be evacuated.* [State the mood of the second clause.]

    5 *Do you think I look fat in this dress?*

Adjectives and adjective groups

In simple terms, an **adjective** is a 'describing word', which tells us something about a person, place or thing (a noun). Adjectives make the meaning of nouns more specific by adding information about size, colour, age, material and many other attributes or qualities.

Adjective groups

In use, adjectives go together to form adjective groups. Note that an adjective group can consist of just one adjective. This is because it has the same function in a sentence as adjective groups consisting of two or more words. The most important word in an adjective group is called its **head**.

An adjective group may consist of :

- a single adjective, eg *hungry*

- co-ordinated adjectives with or without a conjunction, eg *hungry and tired*, *big new*

- an adjective preceded by an adverb, eg *very hungry*

- an adjective followed by a prepositional phrase, eg *hungry for knowledge*

- an adjective followed by a *that*-clause, eg *aware that something was wrong*

- an adjective followed by a *to*-infinitive clause, eg *pleased to see you*.

Two or more adjective groups can be co-ordinated:

> *They were very tired, extremely cold and utterly miserable.*

In other cases, adjectives form part of noun groups (which have a noun or pronoun as the head), eg *a pretty face, time immemorial, something interesting*.

Adjective groups are used as **complements** in a clause.

Adjectives and their positions

Adjectives can often be identified by their endings. Typical adjective endings are *-al*, *-able* or *-ible*, *-ic* or *-ical*, *-ish*, *-ive*, *-ful*, *-less*, *-ous* and *-y*.

Adjectives can be used in one or more of three positions:

- They may come before a noun. This is known as the **attributive** position of adjectives:

> *a green scarf*
>
> *a very old man*
>
> *the enormous spaceship*
>
> *the following day*
>
> *a big strong boy*

Note that some adjectives can only function attributively:

✔ *the bridal suite*	✘ *the suite is bridal*
✔ *my elder brother*	✘ *my brother is elder*
✔ *the sole applicant*	✘ *the applicant is sole*
✔ *an outright lie*	✘ *the lie is outright*

ADJECTIVES AND ADJECTIVE GROUPS

- They may come after a noun and a link verb, eg *be*, *become*, *look*, *seem*, *appear*. This is known as the **predicative** position of adjectives:

> *The house is huge.*
>
> *Harry was cross and bad-tempered.*
>
> *He's getting fat.*
>
> *You're looking very tired.*
>
> *She seemed nervous.*
>
> *I knew I appeared anxious.*

Some adjectives can only function predicatively. These include many adjectives that start with **a-**, eg *afloat*, *afraid*, *alight*, *alive*, *alone*, *asleep*, *awake* and *awash*. Other adjectives like this are: *content*, *due*, *glad*, *ill*, *ready*, *sorry*, *sure*, *well*:

✔ *the fish is alive*	✘ *the alive fish*
✔ *she is awake*	✘ *the awake woman*
✔ *the train is due*	✘ *the due train*
✔ *the dinner is ready*	✘ *the ready dinner*
✔ *I'm really glad*	✘ *a glad person*

Many adjectives that function predicatively can be followed by a **prepositional phrase**, that is, a phrase that consists of a preposition and a noun group:

> *I'm glad about your new job.*
>
> *The drugs were effective against tuberculosis.*
>
> *He said he was open to suggestions.*
>
> *She was inadequate as a mother.*
>
> *He was really mad at me.*

The house is now free of vermin.

I'm not eligible for benefits.

His injuries are consistent with a fall from a great height.

I'm adamant on that point.

He always felt different from his brother.

Many adjectives that function predicatively can also be followed by a *that*-clause:

I was amazed that she spoke to me so rudely.

We were worried that the children were not getting enough vitamins.

Be careful that you don't miss the turning.

I feel very lucky that I have met so many people.

They can also be followed by a *to*-infinitive clause:

They are reluctant to tell the whole truth.

I was helpless to stop the feeling of panic that came over me.

He's certain to win the next election.

Be careful not to eat too much.

● They can be used after a noun, in some cases:

the president elect

since time immemorial

proof positive of his guilt

the heir apparent

presents galore

Notice that these adjectives are mostly used in fixed phrases, and some of them, like *attorney general* and *procurator fiscal*, are often entered in dictionaries as compound nouns.

Certain adjectives are used after a noun when the noun is preceded by an adjective in its superlative form, or by 'the only' or an ordinal number. They may also follow a pronoun like 'something', 'anything' or 'no-one':

> *the shortest time possible*
>
> *the widest gap imaginable*
>
> *the first flight available*
>
> *the only expense allowable*
>
> *He didn't say anything useful.*
>
> *I've got something interesting to show you.*

Most adjectives may be used in both the attributive position and the predicative position. When an adjective can be used in either position it is known as a **central** adjective:

> *the green scarf*   *the scarf is green*
>
> *an infinite number*   *the number is infinite*
>
> *a busy life*   *my life is busy*
>
> *a dangerous man*   *the man is dangerous*

Some adjectives have one meaning when they are used attributively and a different meaning when they are used predicatively. Compare the following examples:

> *My late husband was an army man.*
>
> *Harry's late again.*
>
> *We could just see the faint glow from his torch.*
>
> *I feel faint. Can I have a glass of water, please?*

Comparatives and superlatives

Adjectives can be compared in terms of whether someone or something has more or less of a quality than someone or something else. Only **graded adjectives** (see next section) can be compared in this way.

The **comparative** is used when you are talking about a person or thing that has more of a quality than someone or something else, or than before. The comparative is formed by adding *-er* to the base form, but this is possible only with some adjectives, usually short ones of one or two syllables. For some two-syllable adjectives, or for adjectives of three or more syllables, you use *more* before the adjective. When you want to say that something has less of a quality than someone or something else, or than before, you use *less*:

> *Mary seems to be getting taller every day.*
>
> *Use a fork or a spoon, whichever is easier.*
>
> *The younger boy is only four.*
>
> *Life is getting more and more difficult.*
>
> *We have all become more aware of environmental issues.*
>
> *His column is less interesting these days.*

Comparatives are very often used with 'than':

> *She's two years older than I am.*
>
> *He's more willing than ever to work hard.*
>
> *Swimming at night is more dangerous than at other times.*
>
> *His shirt was a lighter shade of grey than his trousers.*

ADJECTIVES AND ADJECTIVE GROUPS

The **superlative** is used when you are talking about a person or thing that has more of a quality than anything else in a group. The superlative is formed by adding *-est* to the base form, but this is possible only with some adjectives, usually short ones of one or two syllables. For some two-syllable adjectives, or for adjectives of three or more syllables, you use a determiner and then *most* before the adjective. When you want to say that something has less of a quality than anyone or anything else, you use *the least*:

> *My biggest problem is time management.*
>
> *It was the best concert I have ever been to.*
>
> *She's the most beautiful woman in the world.*
>
> *That's the least important point.*

Note that when *most* is used without a determiner or with *a*, it is not superlative but just means 'very':

> *Thank you for your comments. Most interesting!*
>
> *You have made a most important contribution.*

Note that if the base form of the adjective ends in *y*, the *y* is usually changed to *i* when adding the *-er* and *-est* endings.

Some adjectives have comparative and superlative forms, but can also be used with ***more*** or ***most***. Some of these are: ***angry***, ***busy***, ***clever***, ***hungry***, ***likely***, ***narrow***, ***simple***, ***stupid***.

A few adjectives have irregular comparative and superlative forms: *good - better - best*; *bad - worse - worst*. *Old* has two comparatives, *older* and *elder*. *Elder* is used when you are comparing two people, as in *my elder brother*.

Note that a few adjectives, eg *mere* and *late* (in the sense of *recent*), have the superlative forms *merest* and *latest* but no comparative form.

Types of adjective

Adjectives can be divided into several types:

Graded adjectives

A graded adjective is one that is often modified in terms of more or less. For example, we can say that something is *very good*, *quite interesting*, *fairly simple*, *as big as the other one*. Graded adjectives have comparative or superlative forms (see above) or are used with *more* and *the most*.

Graded adjectives are sometimes also called **gradable adjectives**.

Graded adjectives have a number of different meanings in terms of the way they describe nouns. Some of these are:

- the size, speed, age or weight of something:

    the *biggest* problem

    a *fast* car

    an *old* woman

    This suitcase is heavy.

- feelings and attitudes:

    I felt sad.

    an *enthusiastic* worker

    He seemed very worried.

- qualities such as beauty, intelligence, courage etc:

  a very *sensitive* person

  a *silly* girl

  an *honest* worker

  He is very *helpful*.

- the way something looks, tastes, or feels:

  It is rather warm *for the time of year.*

  The soup is too salty.

  a very *clean* room

- how good or bad someone or something is:

  That's good!

  The experience wasn't very pleasant.

  a *horrible* day

Graded adjectives are often modified by **grading adverbs**, which are also known as **adverbs of degree**, eg *a bit*, *awfully*, *fairly*, *too*:

  It's relatively easy *to understand.*

  You're a bit late.

  It's a fairly large *country.*

Grading adverbs are dealt with more fully on pages 98–9.

Ungraded adjectives

Ungraded adjectives describe nouns according to the class or category they belong to. They do not have a comparative or superlative form, and are not used with grading adverbs.

Ungraded adjectives usually come before the noun; many of them
are not used predicatively at all.

Ungraded adjectives are sometimes also called **non-gradable
adjectives**.

Ungraded adjectives also have a number of different meanings in
terms of the way they describe nouns. Some of these are:

- physical position or location:

    my middle finger

    the southern regions

    the opposite corner

- time, duration or frequency:

    the present time

    a permanent position

    regular updates

    the daily newspaper

- age or sex:

    We have two adult children.

    a female cat

- nationality or origin:

    a German woman

    a Russian doll

    French words

- materials:

    a *wooden* floor

    a *woollen* hat

- shape:

    a *square* table

    a *round* coin

- politics, institutions, activities, experience etc.

    They have severed diplomatic links.

    the *presidential* palace

    domestic policy

    criminal activities

Adjectives with graded and ungraded senses

Many adjectives have both graded and ungraded senses. Look at the following pairs:

    scientific research

    His methods are very scientific.

    diplomatic immunity

    You must try to be a bit more diplomatic.

    my *private* life

    He is a very private person.

The first in the pair is ungraded and the second is graded. Some of the other adjectives that behave like this are *civil*, *commercial*, *creative*, *democratic*, *educational*, *false*, *genuine*, *hostile*, *human*, *intelligent*, *late*, *mobile*, *musical*, *nervous*, *original*, *plastic*, *political*, *professional*, *proper*, *public*, *ready*, *simple*, *technical*, *wrong*.

Colour adjectives

Colour adjectives are used to talk about the colour of things. They can be used both attributively and predicatively:

> a shirt with *yellow* and *green* stripes

> *Green* peppers turn *red* as they ripen.

The words *bright*, *dark*, *light*, *deep* and *pale* are used with colour adjectives to indicate the strength or intensity of the colour:

> She wore *bright red* lipstick.

> Bake the pie until the crust is *light brown*.

Many of the more common colour adjectives have comparative and superlative forms:

> The grass is always *greener* on the other side of the fence.

> She has the *whitest* teeth I have ever seen.

Colour adjectives can be preceded by grading adverbs:

> Her teeth were perfect and *extremely white*.

> The sky is *rather grey*. Do you think it will rain?

Note that colours are often nouns as well as adjectives:

> a garish shade of *pink*

> She was dressed in *blue*.

> The room is decorated in *browns* and *beiges*.

Emphasizing or intensifying adjectives

Intensifying or emphasizing adjectives are used before nouns (attributively) to emphasize the quality of something. Some of them are: *absolute*, *complete*, *dead*, *mere*, *outright*, *pure*, *sheer*, *simple*, *total*, *utter*, *very*. Some examples:

> *The party was an* absolute *disaster.*
>
> *I felt like a* complete *idiot.*
>
> *The* mere *thought of it gives me a headache.*
>
> *It was* sheer *lunacy to jump from that height.*
>
> *We lay in the sun all day; it was* total *bliss!*

Participial adjectives

A participial adjective is the *-ing* form (the present participle) or the *-ed* form (the past participle) of a verb that functions as an adjective:

> *a* crying *baby*
>
> *a* startling *revelation*
>
> *a* spent *cartridge*
>
> frozen *peas*
>
> *He's very* depressed.

Compound adjectives

These are adjectives that consist of more than one word, eg *kind-hearted*, *present-day*, *soul-destroying*. (See also page 192.)

Nouns used like adjectives

Many nouns can be used attributively to modify other nouns:

> *a* flower *seller*

a *window* cleaner

the *reptile* house

my *bedroom* slippers

a *winter* coat

a *Russian* speaker

a *passport* holder

a *football* team

a *chicken* casserole

three *milk* bottles

a *coffee* grinder

rock formations

the *bus* stop

The order of adjectives

Two or more adjectives can be used one after another. The usual order is *graded adjective* ▸ *colour adjective* ▸ *ungraded adjective*:

a *big blue* car

beautiful green eyes

a *peaceful democratic* country

a *bleak northern* town

a *damp grey urban* landscape

Adjectives indicating shape, however, may come before colour adjectives:

a *big round green* patch of grass

When two or more graded adjectives are used one after the other, the order is usually *opinions* ▸ *size* ▸ *quality* ▸ *age*:

a *lovely big shiny* bus

a *funny old* man

silly little children

Comparatives and superlatives normally come before all the other adjectives in a noun group:

a *more interesting French* movie

the *best modern Swedish* furniture

the *most popular daily* newspaper

When two or more ungraded adjectives are used one after the other, the order is usually *age* ▸ *shape* ▸ *nationality/origin* ▸ *material*:

an *old French* chapel

a *new rectangular plastic* pot

When a noun group contains noun modifiers (nouns that are used like adjectives), they usually come after the other adjectives:

wide stone steps

a *temporary accountancy* post

an *original Roman mosaic* floor

torn blue denim jeans

Finally, there is a group of words that are sometimes known as **specifying adjectives** or **post-determiners**. These are used to show exactly what you are referring to. Grammarians differ on what should be included in this group, but the point that is usually made about them is that they come after a determiner and before any other adjectives:

the usual lame excuses

the next big thing

the following quick summary

my same old raincoat

a certain old acquaintance of mine

the only good explanation

Some other members of this group are: *additional*, *entire*, *extra*, *final*, *main*, *next*, *other*, *remaining*, *sole*, *whole*.

Checklist

Adjectives describe nouns. The most important adjective in an **adjective group** is known as the head.

1. **An adjective group can consist of:**
   - a single adjective
   - adjectives with conjunctions, adverbs or a prepositional phrase
   - an adjective followed by a *that*-clause or a *to*-infinitive clause

2. **Adjective endings**
   - are often typical, eg *–al*, *-able*, *-ible* etc

3. **Adjective positions:**
   - attributive position: the adjective comes before the noun, eg *the green door*
   - predicative position: the adjective comes after the noun and a link verb, eg *He appeared anxious*
   - both attributive and predicative position: these adjectives are called central adjectives, eg *busy*

- after the noun:
  a. usually occurs in fixed phrases, eg *attorney general*
  b. can occur when the noun is preceded by a superlative, 'the only' or an ordinal number, eg *the only man available*

4. Comparative
- expresses more or greater degree, eg *more difficult*
- can have an irregular form, eg *good - better*

5. Superlative
- expresses the highest degree, eg *least difficult, latest*
- can have an irregular form, eg *good – best*

6. Graded adjectives
- are modified in terms of more or less, eg *good, bad, easy*
- have a comparative and superlative form
- are often modified by grading adverbs, eg *a bit, fairly*

7. Ungraded adjectives
- describe nouns in terms of physical location, age or sex, materials, shape, etc, eg *wooden, German, female*
- do not have a comparative or superlative form

8. Graded and ungraded senses
- some adjectives have graded and ungraded senses, eg *nervous*

9. Colour adjectives
- can be used attributively or predicatively
- can be preceded by grading adverbs, eg *Your face is very red*

10. Emphasizing or intensifying adjectives
- are used attributively to emphasize the quality of something, eg *That is utter stupidity!*

11. Participial adjectives

- are the present or past participles of verbs that function as adjectives, eg an <u>amazing</u> discovery

12. Compound adjectives

- consist of more than one word, eg a <u>well-known</u> author

13. Nouns used like adjectives

- can modify other nouns when placed attributively, eg a <u>summer</u> dress

14. Order of adjectives

a. graded adjective ▶ colour adjective ▶ ungraded adjective

b. comparative or superlative adjectives come before all other adjectives

c. noun adjectives come after all the other adjectives

d. specifying adjectives (or post-determiners) come after a determiner and before any other adjectives, eg a <u>certain</u> old acquaintance of mine

Grammar in practice

A Below are some noun groups where the adjective is in the attributive position. Say which ones can also be used predicatively.

1 *the alleged criminals*

2 *some musical instruments*

3 *a heavy load*

4 *an early start*

5 *the wrong decision*

ADJECTIVES AND ADJECTIVE GROUPS

B Use the adjectives below to fill in the gaps in the following sentences:

particular   cool   famous   eligible   absent

involved   terrified   keen   beneficial   mean

1. *The night air was .... against her skin.*
2. *Birmingham is .... as the home of the industrial revolution.*
3. *Universities need to be more .... in student life.*
4. *Last year he was .... from work for 25 days.*
5. *She was .... of heights.*
6. *I'm very .... about what I eat.*
7. *These plants attract many insects that are .... to the birds.*
8. *They were not .... for government benefits.*
9. *My dad's not too .... on me going away.*
10. *I've always been .... with money.*

C Now do these:

foolish   puzzled   beautiful   lucky   interested

1. *We would be .... to ignore their advice.*
2. *The garden was .... to look at.*
3. *I was .... to find all the doors locked.*
4. *I'd be .... to know what you think about it.*
5. *He was .... to escape with his life.*

Adverbs, adverb groups and adjuncts

An adverb is a word that gives information about how, when, where, why or in what circumstances something happens or is done. For example, *slowly*, *probably*, *frankly* and *briefly* are all adverbs.

Adverb groups

In use, adverbs form adverb groups. An adverb group may consist of a single adverb such as *quickly*, or an adverb preceded by a grading adverb such as *very quickly*. The most important word in an adverb group is called its **head**. Adverb groups function as **adjuncts** in a clause.

The formation of adverbs

Many adverbs are formed from adjectives by adding the ending *-ly* to the adjective. Adverbs formed in this way usually have a meaning that is closely related to the adjective:

adjective	adverb
common	*commonly*
complete	*completely*
foolish	*foolishly*
grave	*gravely*
nervous	*nervously*
fond	*fondly*
narrow	*narrowly*

nice	nicely
hilarious	hilariously

When the adjective ends in *y*, the *y* changes to *i* in the adverb:

adjective	**adverb**
funny	funnily
hasty	hastily
easy	easily
military	militarily
weary	wearily

When an adjective ends in a consonant plus *le*, the final *e* of the adjective is dropped for the adverb, eg *simply*, *doubly*. An exception is *wholly*.

When an adjective ends in a vowel plus *e*, the *e* is sometimes dropped for the adverb, eg *duly*, *truly*, *eerily*.

Adverbs formed from adjectives ending in *ic* have the ending *-ally*, eg *basically*, *frantically*, *specifically*. An exception is *publicly*.

Adverbs formed from adjectives ending in *ll* add *-y* only, eg *fully*, *dully*, *shrilly*.

It is important, however, to remember that not all words ending in *ly* are adverbs. The following is a list of **adjectives** ending in *ly*. These adjectives are never used as adverbs:

beastly	friendly	lowly	sisterly
brotherly	heavenly	manly	timely
costly	lively	masterly	ugly

cowardly	*lonely*	*miserly*	*womanly*
elderly	*lovely*	*silly*	*worldly*

However, some adjectives ending in *ly* are also used as adverbs:

adjective	**adverb**
a *daily* newspaper	newspapers delivered *daily*
an *hourly* bus service	He is paid *hourly*.
a *kindly* man	She treated me *kindly*.
a *leisurely* pace	He bathed *leisurely*.
monthly payments	You will be billed *monthly*.
a *weekly* wage	Are you paid *weekly*?

Some single-word adverbs that do not have the *ly* ending have the same forms as adjectives:

adjective	**adverb**
a *fair* settlement	to play *fair*
a *fast* car	He drives *fast*.
free travel	to travel *free*
hard work	to work *hard*
an *inland* sea	A storm is moving *inland*.
a *long* journey	We didn't stay *long*.

Quick and *slow* are sometimes used as adverbs, though they also have an *ly* form:

> *Eat it quick.*
>
> *Walk quickly.*

Note that some adverbs ending in *ly* do not have the same meaning as the adjectives to which they seem to be related:

adjective	adverb
It was hard work.	*I could hardly recognize him.*
a late arrival	*Have you seen him lately?*
a terrible experience	*I'm terribly worried.*
a short time	*I'll be with you shortly.*

Types of adverb

There are several kinds of adverb. Here we will discuss those that form part of an adjective or adverb group, and which do not function alone as adjuncts in the clause.

Grading adverbs or adverbs of degree

These were discussed briefly on page 84, where we said that grading adverbs are often used with adjectives to form adjective groups, as in *very nice*. They can also be used with other adverbs to form adverb groups, eg *very quickly*, or before adjectives contained in noun groups, eg *a relatively new idea*. They may also come after a verb or at the end of a clause.

Grading adverbs are used to indicate how much of a quality someone or something has. They can indicate a slight or middling degree of something, eg *a bit*, *a little*, *comparatively*, *fairly*, *mildly*, *moderately*, *much*, *pretty*, *quite*, *rather*, *slightly*, *somewhat*:

> *I didn't like him much.*
>
> *It's slightly warmer today.*
>
> *He's reasonably good at his job.*
>
> *I have a fairly good job.*
>
> *She is a relatively quick learner.*
>
> *I thought he spoke rather pompously.*
>
> *I run quite quickly.*

A few of them indicate an equal degree of a quality, eg *as*, *equally*:

> They did *equally* well in the test.

The majority of them indicate that someone or something has a lot of a quality. These are sometimes called **intensifiers**, eg *awfully*, *deeply*, *dreadfully*, *exceedingly*, *excessively*, *extremely*, *highly*, *immensely*, *incredibly*, *infinitely*, *remarkably*, *terribly*, *too*, *unusually*, *very*:

> I'm *awfully* tired.
>
> I'm *dreadfully* sorry.
>
> He's *incredibly* kind.
>
> Chimpanzees are *highly* intelligent.
>
> She has a *remarkably* retentive memory.
>
> He was pedalling *very* fast.
>
> You are walking *too* slowly.

Focusing adverbs

These are used to focus attention on the main thing involved in a situation, eg *chiefly*, *especially*, *exclusively*, *just*, *mainly*, *mostly*, *only*, *particularly*, *primarily*, *purely*, *simply*, *solely*, *specifically*:

> He was *chiefly* responsible for the changes.
>
> I'm *particularly* interested in medieval art.
>
> She was *primarily* involved in bringing up her children.

Some focusing adjectives are used to emphasize that you are only talking about one person or thing:

> *Only* John has a laptop.
>
> He's *solely* responsible for the mess we're in today.

Broad negatives

The adverbs *barely*, *hardly*, *little*, *rarely* and *seldom* are called broad negatives because they are nearly negative in meaning. They always come before the verb:

> *I could* *scarcely* *believe what I was hearing.*
>
> *That's* *hardly* *going to solve our problem.*
>
> *We* *seldom* *entertain.*

Adverb particles

Adverbs that form part of a phrasal verb are known as adverb particles. These include *across*, *aside*, *away*, *back*, *down*, *forward*, *off*, *on*, *out*, *over*, *together*, *up*. They combine with main verbs to form phrasal verbs like *come across*, *look away*, *stand down*, *take off*, *leave out*, *ring up*:

> *You must make* *up* *your mind.*
>
> *I feel as though I've let her* *down.*
>
> *Leave* *out* *any questions you don't understand.*

Compound adverbs

These are adverbs that consist of more than one word, eg *cold-bloodedly*, *good-naturedly*.

Graded and ungraded adverbs

Like adjectives, adverbs can be graded or ungraded. Graded adverbs can be modified in terms of more or less. They are often preceded by a grading adverb (see above):

> *He manages fairly* *successfully.*
>
> *She spoke to us very* *politely.*
>
> *I saw her relatively* *recently.*

She plays extremely confidently.

You may come across the terms **gradable** or **non-gradable adverbs** for **graded** and **ungraded adverbs**.

Graded adverbs can be used in the comparative or superlative. This is normally done using *more* and (*the*) *most*:

> *Speak more loudly.*
>
> *I'd like the invoice to be worked out a bit more accurately.*
>
> *Let's see who can do it the most efficiently.*

As with adjectives, the comparative is also used with 'than':

> *I type more quickly than you do.*
>
> *He treats his children more harshly than he should.*

Adverbs that have the same forms as adjectives also have the same comparative and superlative forms as those adjectives:

> *He drives fast.*
>
> *He drove faster.*
>
> *Which car goes fastest?*

> *We all worked hard.*
>
> *She worked harder.*
>
> *He works hardest in the mornings.*

The split infinitive

A *to*-infinitive is said to be split when an adverb is inserted between the *to* and the verb as in:

>   to *finally* agree
>
>   to *boldly* go

This construction is considered by many people to be unacceptable. However, it is being used more and more, and often it sounds quite natural:

>   *They seem to have* *completely* *won her over.*

Adjuncts

Adverb groups function as adjuncts in a clause, eg *happily*, *quickly*, *quite happily*, *rather interestingly*. So do prepositional phrases, eg *with care*, *for the time being*, and occasionally noun groups, eg *next year*. There are several different types of adjunct:

Adjuncts of manner

These answer the question 'How?':

>   *Run* *quickly* *and fetch your father.*
>   *Sophie stared* *moodily* *into the distance.*
>   *He asked how I was getting on* *workwise*.
>   *We are not playing* *well enough*.
>   *You're driving* *too fast*.
>   *The label said 'Handle* *with care'*.

Adjuncts of place

These answer the question 'Where?', 'Where to?', or 'Where from?':

>   *She felt as if she was getting* *nowhere*.
>   *We had to walk* *home*.
>   *There he is,* *over there*.

How are you travelling to Frankfurt?

The man on the left is the ambassador.

He flew in from New York.

Adjuncts of duration

These answer the question 'How long?':

She can't keep this up indefinitely.

He glanced at me very briefly.

He works from nine to five.

Let's leave that to one side for the time being.

Adjuncts of time

These answer the question 'When?'. Some do not refer to a definite time:

Are you working tomorrow?

Nowadays, salmon is usually farmed.

Have you seen Jon recently?

He'll be fifty next April.

Those books you ordered have come at last.

Adjuncts of frequency

These answer the question 'How often?':

Will I be paid weekly or monthly?

I never go out on weekday evenings.

Every year we have a holiday in the sun.

I visited her from time to time.

Adjuncts of aspect

These are used when you want to make it clear what aspect of something you are talking about, or from what point of view you are considering something:

> *The plan is not commercially viable.*
>
> *Has this been scientifically proven?*
>
> *Technically speaking, the programme is very complex.*
>
> *From a political point of view, I agree with you.*

Sentence adjuncts

These modify a whole clause or sentence but stand outside its grammatical structure. They are usually separated from the main part of the sentence by a comma (when the sentence adjunct comes at the beginning of a sentence) or a pair of commas (when it comes in the middle of a sentence). Sentence adjuncts are usually adverb groups, though occasionally a prepositional phrase is used.

The main function of a sentence adjunct is to indicate your reaction to, or opinion of, the fact or event that you are talking about. Some sentence adjuncts of this type are *astonishingly, characteristically, coincidentally, fortunately, happily, incredibly, interestingly, ironically, luckily, mercifully, naturally, oddly, of course, predictably, sadly, typically, unfortunately*:

> *Luckily, I managed to see her before she left.*
>
> *Quite surprisingly, my mother refused to help me.*
>
> *Mercifully, we didn't have to wait for long*
>
> *Unfortunately, I won't be able to come tonight.*
>
> *He let me down, predictably, but I soon got over it.*
>
> *Funnily enough, I dreamt about you last night.*

Some sentence adjuncts tell your listener or reader how to interpret what you are saying, eg *briefly*, *candidly*, *confidentially*, *frankly*, *foolishly*, *honestly*, *literally*, *normally*, *in general*:

> *Frankly, my dear, I don't give a damn.*
>
> *Honestly, I couldn't help it.*
>
> *Foolishly, I didn't ask to see his ID before I let him in.*
>
> *Normally, I would have asked to see some form of identification.*
>
> *In general, she was confused about what she wanted to do.*

Linking adjuncts

These adjuncts are used to connect one clause or sentence with another. They are usually adverb groups, though occasionally a prepositional phrase is used. There are four main types:

- They can indicate **sequence**, showing when something happened or will happen, or the order in which things take place, eg *afterwards*, *beforehand*, *eventually*, *finally*, *in the end*, *last*, *later*, *next*, *previously*, *soon*, *subsequently*, *then*. You can also use one of these adjuncts to indicate that something takes place at the same time as something else: *meanwhile*, *in the meantime*, *simultaneously*:

> *The police eventually caught up with him.*
>
> *I'll add the footnotes last of all.*
>
> *When I saw him next, he was married.*
>
> *We tried, but in the end we had to give up.*

- They can be used for **making a list** or **adding information**, eg *also*, *besides*, *finally*, *first*, *furthermore*, *moreover*, *next*, *secondly*, *too*. The adjunct may be a prepositional phrase such as *on top of that*:

> *She is a crime writer. Also, she has written her autobiography.*
>
> *And finally, let me announce the winner.*
>
> *You've been late every day this week. And on top of that, you haven't done your coursework.*

- They can be used for **contrasting** two or more things or giving alternatives, eg *alternatively, conversely, however, instead, nevertheless, on the contrary, on the other hand, rather, still, then again, though.*

> *She could have tried to keep the room tidy; instead, it was littered with clothes and toys.*
>
> *I don't much like him. I admit he's very attractive, though.*
>
> *The idea is not likely to unite us. On the contrary, I think it will divide us.*

- They can be used to indicate the result of something, eg *accordingly, as a result, consequently, hence, so, therefore, thus:*

> *He broke his back when he was 60. Consequently, he had to spend the rest of his life in a wheelchair.*
>
> *He committed a crime, so he went to jail.*
>
> *The stock market is still falling, and as a result, people's pension funds are shrinking.*

The order of adjuncts

Adjuncts of manner, place and time usually come after the main verb, in that order. If the verb has an object, they come after the object:

The baby was whimpering pathetically [manner] *in her cot* [place] *all morning* [time].

You can also put an adjunct of manner before a main verb:

She quickly *made up her mind to leave.*

Checklist

Adverbs give information about how, when, where, why or in what circumstances something happens or is done. The most important word in an adverb group is called its head. **Adverb groups** function as adjuncts in a clause.

1. **Adverbs are usually formed by:**
- adding *–ly*, *-ally* or *y* to adjectives, often changing the spelling, eg *cleverly*, *simply*, *basically*

2. **Adverbs ending in** *ly*
- do not always have the same meaning as the adjective from which they are derived, eg *hard/hardly*

3. **Adjectives ending in** *ly*
- are not always used as adverbs, eg *beastly*

4. **Adverbs that do not end in** *ly*
- have the same form as the adjective, eg *long*

5. **Grading adverbs (or adverbs of degree)**
- are used to indicate how much of a quality someone or something has
- are often used with adjectives or adverbs, eg <u>*very*</u> *big*
- can be used before adjectives in noun groups, eg *a* <u>*fairly*</u> *old man*
- may come after a verb, eg *He limped* <u>*slightly*</u>

6. Intensifiers
- are grading adverbs that indicate that someone or something has a lot of a quality, eg *extremely*

7. Focusing adverbs
- focus attention on the main thing, eg *especially*, *chiefly*

8. Broad negatives
- are nearly negative in meaning, eg *barely*

9. Adverb particles
- are adverbs that form part of a phrasal verb, eg *take off*

10. Compound adverbs
- consist of more than one word, eg *good-humouredly*

11. Graded adverbs
- can be modified in terms of more or less, eg *successful*
- are often preceded by a grading adverb

12. Ungraded adverbs
- cannot be modified and do not have a comparative or superlative form, eg *mortally*, *finally*
- are often adverbs of degree, eg *very*, *slightly* etc

13. Split infinitive
- occurs when an adverb is placed between *to* and the verb in a to-infinitive, eg *to quickly disappear*

14. Adjuncts
- give information on how and where something is done as well as duration, time, frequency and aspect

15. Sentence adjuncts
- modify a whole sentence or clause and are separated from the main part of the sentence by a comma or a pair of commas

- usually indicate a reaction to, or opinion about, a fact or event

16. Linking adjuncts
- connect one clause or sentence with another
- can indicate result or when an action takes place, eg *consequently*, *meanwhile*
- can be used for contrast or adding information eg *however*, *furthermore*

17. Order of adjuncts
- main verb followed by adjuncts of manner, place and time
- adjunct of manner can come before the main verb

Grammar in practice

A Use the adverbs below to fill in the gaps in the following sentences:

> *commonly   happily   easily   monthly   recently*
>
> *narrowly   well   quietly   sadly   carefully*

1 *Chocolate is the most .... craved food.*

2 *............... I have tried my hand at portrait painting.*

3 *We .... defeated the opposition.*

4 *Scientists have been working .... behind the scenes.*

5 *Our married life continued .... for six years.*

6 *I went to the graveyard of my dearly loved and .... missed husband.*

7 *Cook until tender or until a fork goes in ....*

8 *You should drive very .... in frosty weather.*

9 *The journal is published ....*

10 *I play the guitar, though not very ....*

B State which kind of adjunct has been used in the following sentences (manner, place, duration, time, frequency, aspect, linking, or sentence adjunct):

1 *He agreed with some reluctance.*

2 *Jurors are only rarely permitted to know about a defendant's past crimes.*

3 *We are enjoying a successful year financially.*

4 *His wife was anxiously waiting for his return.*

5 *Basically, I was advising him to pay off his debts.*

6 *The department is facing a lot of problems these days.*

7 *'Don't tramp mud everywhere,' said his father.*

8 *The data collection, therefore, needs to be as rapid as possible.*

9 *She sleeps from about noon to nine at night.*

10 *She didn't run away; instead she tried to get back into the house.*

Pronouns

Pronouns are a closed word class. They differ from nouns in that they do not have adjectives before them, and they are not preceded by determiners like *a*, *an* or *the*.

Pronouns as substitutes for noun groups

The following examples demonstrate how pronouns are used as substitutes for noun groups:

> *Alice doesn't live here any longer.*
> *She doesn't live here any longer.*
>
> *He trains dogs.*
> *He trains them.*
>
> *A famous barrister has agreed to represent them.*
> *He has agreed to represent them.*
>
> *My parents will meet us at the station.*
> *They will meet us at the station.*

In the first example, the pronoun *she* replaces the noun group 'Alice'; in the second, the pronoun *them* replaces the noun group 'dogs'; in the third, the pronoun *he* replaces the noun group 'a famous barrister'; and in the fourth, the pronoun *they* replaces the noun group 'my parents'. (Note that 'Alice' and 'dogs' are considered to be noun groups even though they only contain one word.)

Pronouns are often used when someone or something has been

mentioned already, and the repetition of the same words would create a stilted effect. Compare the following examples:

Jane phoned earlier. Would you phone Jane back?

Jane phoned earlier. Would you phone her back?

The goalkeeper dived for the ball. The goalkeeper missed the ball.

The goalkeeper dived for the ball. He missed it.

Pronouns that do not replace a noun group

There are some cases where pronouns do not act as substitutes for a noun group. In conversation, the pronouns *I* and, occasionally, *one* are used by the speaker, and the pronoun *you* is used for the person or people being spoken to. *We* is also used instead of *I* in written English, for example in textbooks. These pronouns do not therefore replace nouns, as is illustrated in the following examples:

I told you about this before.

You are more qualified than I am.

As we pointed out in section 6 …

Similarly, when the pronoun *it* is inserted as a 'dummy' subject in a clause containing a **finite** verb, it does not replace a noun group. It is used in this way because a finite verb needs a subject. (Finite verb groups are discussed more fully on pages 68–9.) *It* is used as a dummy subject in the following examples:

What time is it?

It's getting rather cold in the evenings now.

It would be foolish to argue with him.

It seems that I was right.

It doesn't matter what you think.

It sounds as if they made a mistake.

Types of pronoun

Pronouns can be grouped into several types. The first three types, **personal**, **possessive** and **reflexive pronouns**, have both singular and plural forms. Also, these three types of pronoun are the only words in English in which grammatical gender differences occur: that is, they have masculine, feminine and 'neuter' forms.

Personal pronouns

Personal pronouns refer to people or things. They can be used as the subject, object or complement of a clause, and their form changes according to the role they play in the clause.

The following forms can be used as the subject of a clause:

	singular	plural
first person	I	we
second person	you	you
third person masculine	he	they
third person feminine	she	they
third person 'neuter'	it	they

The following forms can be used as the object of a clause:

	singular	plural
first person	me	us
second person	you	you
third person masculine	him	them
third person feminine	her	them
third person 'neuter'	it	them

PRONOUNS

In addition to the pronouns listed above, *one* is also used as a personal pronoun. It is sometimes used as a substitute for *I*, though this is now considered rather formal and old-fashioned. *One* or *you* is used to refer to people in a general way:

> *One* can't be too careful.
>
> *You* can't beat a nice cold lager.

They is also used in expressions such as 'they say' to refer vaguely to people in general when you are making statements about what people say, think or do:

> *They* keep putting the prices up.
>
> *They* say he's a loser.

The following examples show how personal pronouns are used as subjects and objects:

subject	object
I need a holiday.	Bob phoned *me*.
You must be joking.	I can't hear *you*.
He has a new job.	I'll email *him* today.
She's a good cook.	Do you believe *her*?
It won't budge.	I bought *it* in Leeds.
We ran all the way.	They beat *us*.
You can all join in.	He loves *you* both.
They come from India.	Did you find *them*?

Note that the object form is also used after a preposition:

> Jack came with *me*.
>
> Give it to *her*.
>
> There isn't much difference between *them* and *us*.

The second person singular *you* is unchanged for the second person plural both when it is a subject and when it is an object. For this reason, the second person plural is often used with a word like *any* or *both*, to make it clear that more than one person is being addressed:

> *You can all join in.*
>
> *I'd like you both to come.*

A personal pronoun can also be used as a complement after the verb *to be*:

> *Oh, it's you. What a surprise!*
>
> *That's it!*
>
> *Of course, the person who'll have to do all the work is me.*
>
> *It is not we who are to blame.*
>
> *It was I who made the complaint.*

Look at the last two examples. Although in formal English you would use *we* and *I* here, it would be just about acceptable in more informal situations to use an object pronoun:

> *It is not us who are to blame.*
>
> *It was me who made the complaint.*

It is even more acceptable to use the object pronoun if it is not linked to another clause:

> *It was me.*

When two or more personal pronouns are linked, the order is usually third person plus second person plus first person:

> *You and she will never get along.*

I expect Paul will have presents for you and me.

He, you and I have joint responsibility.

When a noun and a personal pronoun are linked by *and* to form a noun group, and this noun group is the subject of the verb, you should use the subject pronoun. When the noun group is the object of the verb, you should use the object pronoun. It is a common error to use the wrong pronoun, as is shown in the following examples:

✗ *The girls and me saw that film last week.*

✔ *The girls and I saw that film last week.*

✗ *Neil and him went swimming this morning.*

✔ *Neil and he went swimming this morning.*

✗ *You must tell Mum and I as soon as you know anything.*

✔ *You must tell Mum and me as soon as you know anything.*

Usage

A simple way of checking whether you are using the correct form of the pronoun is to take away the words linked to the pronoun and see if the clause or statement then reads properly.

If you apply this test to the first of the pairs of examples given above, you will see immediately that the wrong form of the pronoun has been used:

✗ *Me saw that film last week.*

✗ *Him went swimming this morning.*

✗ *You must tell I as soon as you know anything.*

After the conjunction *but*, you use either the subject or object pronoun when it comes before a verb. When the pronoun is at the end of the clause, you use the object pronoun:

> *No one but he can open the vault.*
>
> *No one but him can open the vault.*
>
> *No one can open the vault but him.*

There is sometimes doubt about which pronoun to use after words like *as* and *than*. In formal English, the subject pronoun is used, but in informal contexts and increasingly also in formal ones, the object pronoun can be used:

> *He is as clever as I am.* [formal]
>
> *He is as clever as me.* [informal]
>
> *She works harder than he does.* [formal]
>
> *She works harder than him.* [informal]

Possessive pronouns

Possessive pronouns, as their name suggests, are used to show who or what something belongs to or is associated with. Like the personal pronouns, the possessive pronouns have singular and plural forms and masculine and feminine forms:

	singular	**plural**
first person	mine	ours
second person	yours	yours
third person masculine	his	theirs
third person feminine	hers	theirs

> *Is this cup of coffee yours or mine?*

I'm using my husband's car today. Mine's in the garage.

It's your job to make sure the work is done on time, not hers.

If you don't have a drill, Raymond can lend you his.

We had to search through a huge pile of bags before we found ours.

All the land as far as you can see is theirs.

Possessive pronouns can be used after *of*:

She's a friend of mine.

I read a book of his.

Note that there is no possessive pronoun *its*. You can say '*its* engine' where *its* is a possessive determiner (see page 135) but you cannot say 'The engine is *its*.'

Do not use an apostrophe before the *s* in the possessive pronouns *yours*, *hers*, *ours* and *theirs*.

Reflexive pronouns

Reflexive pronouns are used to relate back to the subject. They have masculine, feminine and 'neuter' forms, as well as singular and plural forms.

	singular	**plural**
first person	myself	ourselves
second person	yourself	yourselves
third person masculine	himself	themselves
third person feminine	herself	themselves
third person 'neuter'	itself	themselves

A reflexive pronoun is used as the object or indirect object of a clause when it refers back to the subject:

> *I asked myself what was going on.*
>
> *You must look after yourself properly.*
>
> *Treat yourselves to a bottle of wine with your dinner.*
>
> *We sat round the fire to keep ourselves warm.*
>
> *Winter was coming, so she knitted herself a scarf.*

A reflexive pronoun may be used after a preposition:

> *They were feeling very proud of themselves.*
>
> *We tried to take him out of himself.*
>
> *She looked at herself in every mirror she passed.*
>
> *The children were talking among themselves.*

Oneself is also a reflexive pronoun. It is sometimes used as a formal substitute for *myself*. *Oneself* or *yourself* is also used to refer to people in a general way:

> *It is no more than one would demand of oneself.*
>
> *It is not always possible to protect yourself against loss in these circumstances.*

Reflexive pronouns and verbs

There are certain verbs that are often or always used with a reflexive pronoun, eg *avail*, *busy*, *content*, *enjoy*, *exert*, *pride*:

> *I availed myself of every opportunity to get a good education.*
>
> *She was busying herself in the kitchen.*
>
> *Just content yourself with what you have.*
>
> *Try not to exert yourselves too much.*

They enjoyed themselves immensely last night.

The company prides itself on its efficiency.

With some verbs the reflexive pronoun is optional but is usually included when you want to emphasize that the subject is capable of performing the action independently. Equally, it may be omitted when it is already obvious that the subject is performing the action on himself, herself or itself:

He was so weak that he couldn't shave or dress himself.

Why is the dog scratching itself? Has it got fleas?

Laura's been able to bath herself since she was three.

But:

He has gone upstairs to shave.

Reflexive pronouns used for emphasis

Reflexive pronouns are also used after nouns or pronouns to emphasize them:

I want to speak to the manager himself, not his secretary.

I myself have never heard of him.

The village itself was very small.

They are also used at the end of a clause to emphasize the subject:

I don't enjoy cooking much, myself.

Interrogative pronouns

The interrogative pronouns are *who*, *whom*, *whose*, *which* and *what*. Except for *what*, they are also relative pronouns (see below), and *which*, *whose* and *what* are also determiners (see page 143). Interrogative pronouns are used for asking questions about people or things. Note that the words *how*, *when*, *why* and *where* are also used for asking questions about manner, time, reason and place, but they are considered to be adverbs rather than pronouns.

You use *who* when you are asking about someone's identity. *Who* can be the subject, object or complement of a clause:

> *Who's making the coffee this morning? (subject)*
>
> *Who did you invite? (object)*
>
> *Who was that on the phone? (complement)*

In formal contexts, *whom* is often used instead of *who* when it is the object of a clause:

> *Whom did you invite?*
>
> *Whom shall we contact about this matter?*

Who is often used instead of *whom* when the clause ends with a preposition:

> *Who do I make the cheque out to?*

However, *whom* is always used when it follows a preposition:

> ✔ *To whom do I make out the cheque?*
>
> ✗ *To who do I make out the cheque?*

PRONOUNS

Whose is used when you are asking questions about who something belongs to:

> *That one is definitely mine. But* whose *is this?*
>
> *I seem to have Jamie's socks.* Whose *have you got?*

Which and *what* are used for asking questions about things. They can be the subject, object or complement of a clause:

> Which *came first, the chicken or the egg? (subject)*
>
> Which *do you prefer, tea or coffee? (object)*
>
> Which *is the cheapest? (complement)*

> What *makes the tides rise and fall? (subject)*
>
> What *does this little gadget do? (object)*
>
> What *is his exact role in the company? (complement)*

Which can also be used to ask for the identity of one out of a group of people:

> Which *of them got the best marks?*

Relative pronouns

The relative pronouns are *who*, *whom*, *whose*, *which*, *that*, *when* and *where*. (*Who*, *whom*, *whose* and *which* are also interrogative pronouns, as explained above.) The clause that follows a relative pronoun is called a **relative clause**.

Who and *whom* are used when you are referring to people. *Which* is used to refer to things, and *that* is used to refer to both people and things. *Whose* is used to talk about possession. *When* is used to refer to time, and *where* is used to refer to place.

The person who can deal with your enquiry isn't here today.

These are the friends whom I met in Glasgow.

The model which you chose is out of stock.

He always had the best that money can buy.

He is the man that can make your problems disappear.

He could remember a time when he had no trouble getting up in the morning.

Details are available from the travel agent where you booked your holiday.

A relative pronoun usually comes at the beginning of a relative clause, and can be the subject or object of the relative clause:

I had a car that just wouldn't start in the mornings. (subject)

I had a car that I just couldn't seem to start. (object)

The relative pronouns *whom* and *which* can also be used after a preposition:

The house, of which they are very proud, is beautifully furnished.

The relative pronoun *whom* can only be used as the object of the clause. It is used in formal contexts instead of the more informal *who*:

My aunt, whom I love dearly, is in hospital. [formal]

My aunt, who I love dearly, is in hospital. [informal]

Whom has to be used instead of *who* when the relative pronoun is preceded by a preposition:

My assistant, in whom I have complete confidence, will be organizing the event.

Whose is a bit different from the other relative pronouns, in that it does not occur on its own, but always comes before a noun:

Peter, whose house I'm living in, is in prison for two years.

People whose tickets are numbered 1–34 can board now.

The relative pronoun is often omitted when it is the object of the relative clause, and when no ambiguity would result from its omission, as in:

The person (who) you want isn't in the office today.

I really like the suit (that) you were wearing yesterday.

For more information on relative clauses, see pages 182–3.

Demonstrative pronouns

The demonstrative pronouns are *this*, *that*, *these* and *those*. The singular forms are *this* and *that*, and the plural forms are *these* and *those*. Note that the demonstrative pronouns also function as determiners (see pages 134–5).

The demonstrative pronouns are used to refer to relative position in space and in time. *This* and *these* indicate closeness, while *that* and *those* indicate a longer distance:

Would you read this to me? I can't find my glasses.

Look at that man over there – he has green hair.

Right, these are the linguistics books, and those are all crime fiction.

The demonstrative pronouns are used to refer to things. It is not polite to use them to refer to people except when identifying oneself or someone else, especially on the telephone, or when making introductions:

> *Hi, is* that *you, Paul?* This *is Phoebe.*
>
> *Was* that *the meter reader at the door?*
>
> *Who's* this*? She looks very like you.*
>
> This *is my colleague, Tom Betts.*

Indefinite pronouns

Indefinite pronouns are of three types.

- **Group 1**

anybody	everybody	somebody	nobody
anyone	everyone	someone	no one (or no-one)
anything	everything	something	nothing

These pronouns are used to refer to people or things without saying who or which they are. The indefinite pronouns referring to a person or people end in *one* or *body*. Both forms have the same meaning and can be used interchangeably, though those that end in *one* are more frequent. A singular verb is used with members of this group of indefinite pronouns.

> *He was too frightened to tell* anyone*.*
>
> *There isn't* anything *we can do.*
>
> *Not* everyone *agrees with you.*
>
> *He was a man who had* everything*.*
>
> *I need* someone *to help me.*
>
> *There's* something *I need to ask you.*
>
> *Sometimes I feel* no one *cares.*

That's nothing to do with me.

You can use an adjective after an indefinite pronoun:

Someone famous is visiting the town.

There's nothing funny about this at all.

Although the indefinite pronouns used to refer to people are followed by a singular verb, the plural pronouns *they*, *them* and *themselves* are often used to refer back to the indefinite pronoun. This is to avoid the expressions 'he or she', 'his and hers' and 'himself and herself', which many people now regard as formal and awkward-sounding:

Nobody should leave unless they have permission.

Everyone gets a locker for their personal belongings.

Anyone who hurts themselves should stop the training programme immediately.

- **Group 2**

  These express a range of meanings, such as the inclusive meanings of words like *all* and *each*, and the negative meaning of words like *none* and *least*. Members of this group include *all*, *another*, *any*, *both*, *each*, *enough*, *a few/fewer/fewest*, *half*, *a little/less/least*, *many*, *most*, *much*, *none*, *several*, *some*:

  The workers were given a series of tests. All were declared fit.

  I thought there was a whole packet of biscuits but someone's eaten half.

  I looked for information but found none.

  Do you want salad, or chips, or both?

Many of the pronouns in this group are also used as determiners.

- **Group 3**

  There are only two pronouns in this group: *either* and *neither*. They are used when referring to alternatives and choices. Again they may be used alone or followed by *of*:

  Do either of you smoke or drink?

  They waved goodbye; neither seemed to mind that I was leaving.

Reciprocal pronouns

The reciprocal pronouns are *each other* and *one another*. They express a reciprocal or mutual relationship between two or more people:

The mothers in the group help and support each other.

You and Fenella know one another, don't you?

Checklist

Pronouns are words usually used as a substitute for a noun or noun group. They are not preceded by adjectives or determiners such as *a*, *an* or *the*.

1. **Pronouns used as substitutes for noun groups**
   - can replace singular or plural nouns
   - are usually used to avoid the repetition of a word

2. **Pronouns that do not replace a noun group**
   - are used in speech or textbooks, eg *We will discuss this in detail in the next chapter*
   - are used in clauses containing a finite verb that requires a subject, eg *It will be dark soon*

3. Personal pronouns

- refer to people or things, and can have singular or plural forms eg *you*, *she*, *they*
- can be used as the subject, object or complement of a clause, eg *I need to go*; *he called <u>me</u>*
- can be used as a complement after the verb to be, eg *Oh it's you!*

4. Subject pronouns and object pronouns

- the form of the pronoun depends on whether it is the subject or object of the clause, eg *He called Joe and <u>me</u>* but *Joe and <u>I</u> went swimming*
- when the pronoun is at the end of the clause after the conjunction *but*, the object pronoun is used, eg *Nobody has the combination but <u>him</u>*
- after the words *like* or *as*, it is more correct to use the subject pronoun, but in informal contexts, the object pronoun is widely used, eg *He is as clever as <u>me</u>*

5. Possessive pronouns

- are used to indicate who or what something belongs to, eg *hers*, *theirs*
- do not have an apostrophe

6. Reflexive pronouns

- relate back to the subject, eg *She washed <u>herself</u>*
- have singular and plural forms, as well as masculine, feminine and neuter, eg *itself*, *themselves*
- may be used after a preposition, eg *He talked to <u>himself</u>*
- are always used after certain verbs, such as *avail*
- can be used after nouns or pronouns for emphasis, eg *I wanted to see the manager <u>herself</u>*

7. Interrogative pronouns: *who*, *whom*, *whose*, *which* and *what*

- are used for asking questions about people or things

8. **Relative pronouns:** *who, whom, whose, which, that, when* and *where*
- are followed by a relative clause, eg *The girl <u>who</u> recited the poem won the prize*
- can be the subject or object of the relative clause
- are often omitted when they are the object of the relative clause, eg *The girl (whom) you saw is my sister*

9. **Demonstrative pronouns:** *this, that, these* and *those*
- refer to relative position in space and time
- refer to things

10. **Indefinite pronouns**
- can be used to refer to people or things without specifying them, eg *anybody, something*
- can be used to express inclusiveness or the opposite, eg *all, none*
- can be used to refer to choices or alternatives, eg *either, neither*

11. **Reciprocal pronouns:** *each other* and *one another*
- express a mutual relationship, eg *They knew <u>one another</u>*

Grammar in practice

A Fill in the gaps in the following sentences with an appropriate personal pronoun:

1 *He always embarrasses ………. in front of my friends.*

2 *Jane and Sue didn't like each other much; ………. were always quarrelling.*

3 *Mum said she would let ………. play by ourselves.*

    4 *As for Jason, I've seen nothing of .... since the funeral.*

    5 *Martha knew what .... wanted and said so.*

B Fill in the gaps in the following sentences with an appropriate possessive pronoun:

    1 *He looked at me quickly, his eyes meeting ....*

    2 *If you take one of ours, we'll take one of ....*

    3 *She wears glasses like Grace, but .... have steel rims instead of brown ones.*

    4 *Leopards can't change their spots, but butterflies can shed .... with surprising ease.*

    5 *That galaxy is millions of light years away from ....*

C These sentences all contain the wrong relative pronoun. In each case, say what it should be:

    1 *His wife was Mary, a nurse, to who he was absolutely devoted.*

    2 *He was the man which was responsible for the mistakes.*

    3 *I made friends with a girl that father ran the ice-cream stall.*

    4 *It was music the likes of that he had never heard in his life.*

    5 *I pray for a day where nuclear weapons will no longer exist.*

Determiners

Determiners are a closed word class. They are used before nouns to indicate whether you are referring to a particular thing or to something of a particular type.

There are two main types of determiner: **specific determiners** and **general determiners**. There are also three smaller groups: **exclamative determiners**, **interrogative determiners** and **pre-determiners**.

Specific determiners

You use a specific determiner when you are referring to a specific person or thing. The specific determiners are the **definite article** *the*, the **demonstrative determiners** like *this* and *that*, and the **possessive determiners** like *my* and *his*. Only one specific determiner can be used before a noun, though you can use a specific determiner followed by a general determiner.

Definite article

The definite article is the word *the*. It is used before singular and plural count nouns, and before uncount nouns.

The definite article is used:

● when you are referring for a second time to a person or thing that you have already mentioned:

A shepherd was driving a large flock of sheep down the middle of the road with the help of two eager-looking collie dogs. *The* shepherd opened a gate in the hedge and *the* collies skilfully directed *the* sheep through *the* narrow gap.

* when you are referring to people and things and your hearer or reader is expected to know which particular person or thing you mean:

   I'm taking the children to the dentist tomorrow.

   What's wrong with the cat?

   You'll find antiseptic in the bathroom.

* before a noun which is followed by a relative clause or prepositional phrase that specifies or identifies which particular person or thing you mean:

   I want to speak to the person who deals with loan applications.

   The bread I bought yesterday has gone hard already.

   What's the function of the key with F1 on it?

* before a singular count noun when you are referring to an entire class or species rather than a particular member of that class or species:

   Life would be very different without the mobile phone.

   Outside national parks, the gorilla is threatened with extinction.

   As a rule, the village policeman sees fewer serious crimes than his urban counterpart.

* before a word that is usually an adjective but which can also be used with *the* to give a collective label to a group of people, eg *the unemployed*, *the underprivileged*, *the rich*, *the poor*, *the sick*. In the same way it can be used to refer

to people of a particular nationality, eg *the Swedish*, *the Welsh*.

- before the names of some countries whose name is plural or includes the words *kingdom*, *union* or *republic*, eg *the Netherlands*, *the United Kingdom*, *the Czech Republic*. You also use it for seas and oceans, rivers, islands and island groups, mountain ranges and deserts, eg *the North Sea*, *the Atlantic*, *the Ganges*, *the Isle of Man*, *the Azores*, *the Andes*, *the Sahara*.

- before the names of public buildings and institutions, hotels, hospitals, museums, pubs etc, and also before the names of some newspapers and magazines, eg *the Tower of London*, *the Stock Exchange*, *the Hilton*, *the Children's Hospital*, *the National Gallery*, *the Queen Victoria*, *the Guardian*, *the Evening Standard*, *the Spectator*. But not all of these are used with the definite article, eg *Tate Modern*, *Cosmopolitan*.

- instead of a possessive determiner to refer in an impersonal way to a part of a person's body:

  He was punched in the stomach.

  We may have to remove the appendix.

The definite article is not often used before names or titles of people, except in the following cases:

- when you are using the plural form of a family's surname to refer collectively to members of that family:

  the legendary feud between the Campbells and the Macdonalds

  The Smiths from across the road have invited us to their party.

DETERMINERS

- when you want to make it clearly understood that the person you are talking about is the one that everyone has heard of and is not to be confused with anyone else of the same name. Note that the definite article is always stressed in this case:

> Surely you don't mean _the_ David Beckham was there?

Demonstrative determiners

The demonstrative determiners are *this*, *that*, *these* and *those*. They come before a noun. *This* and *that* are the singular forms and are used before singular count nouns, uncount nouns and 'one'. *These* and *those* are the plural forms and are used before plural count nouns and 'ones'.

The demonstrative determiners are used to indicate relative position in space and in time. *This* and *these* are used when indicating something that is relatively close or near; *that* and *those* are used to indicate something that is a greater distance away.

> **i**
>
> Remember that all the words used as demonstrative determiners also function as pronouns.

The following examples show the use of demonstrative determiners:

> *This* mug is dirty. See if *that* one on the draining board is clean.
>
> Are you doing anything *this* Friday?
>
> What do you remember about *that* day?
>
> You know who I mean – *that* lad with the red hair.
>
> One of *these* scarves must be yours.
>
> *These* chips are cold.
>
> What are *those* buildings over there?

Those big chimneys are going to be knocked down soon.

You can also use *that* when you are referring to something that has just happened:

That accident looked serious.

In informal speech, the determiners *this* and *these* may also be used in front of nouns even when you are mentioning someone or something for the first time. In other words, they function more like general determiners:

This woman came up to me in the street and asked me where I had bought my jacket.

There was this enormous bloke standing in front of me and I couldn't see a thing.

She had on these baggy trousers that looked like something Charlie Chaplin might wear.

Possessive determiners

Possessive determiners can be either singular or plural. They may be masculine or feminine, and there is also a 'neuter' form. In this they differ from possessive pronouns (see page 118), which have no 'neuter' form.

	singular	plural
first person	my	our
second person	your	your
third person masculine	his	their
third person feminine	her	their
third person 'neuter'	its	their

Possessive determiners are used when referring to something that belongs to someone:

I had an accident and my car is in the garage.

Did you come here on your bicycle?

Raymond says you can borrow his lawnmower.

She took off her shoes.

What has that magpie got in its beak?

We had a long wait for our luggage.

Their land stretches as far as you can see.

Possessive determiners do not have to refer to something that is owned. They can simply refer to something that is connected or associated with someone or something, or to an action in order to indicate who or what is doing it:

It is your job to make sure the work is done on time.

I don't think it was her fault.

He always teased his little brother.

We must respect our history and culture.

The yachts are all safely tied up in their berths.

I waited impatiently for her arrival.

He has lost his fight for life.

If you want to emphasize that something belongs to or is closely associated with someone, you can use *own* after the determiner:

I saw it with my own eyes.

He took his own life.

I wanted to manage my own affairs.

We're moving into our own house next week.

General determiners

You use a general determiner when you are referring to someone or something for the first time, or when you are talking about them in general terms.

The general determiners are:

a	another	enough	least	most	several
a few	any	every	less	much	some
a little	both	few	little	neither	
all	each	fewer	many	no	
an	either	fewest	more	other	

Indefinite article

A and *an* are the most frequent general determiners, often called the **indefinite articles**. The indefinite article is used before a count noun to refer to things and people in a general or indefinite way. Specifically, it is used:

- when you are mentioning someone or something for the first time:

    I was reading a book when she phoned.

    He wants to buy a flat.

    She met an old friend yesterday.

- when you are making a general statement about all people or things of a particular type:

137

A computer can store and retrieve huge amounts of information.

A cat is not such a good companion as a dog.

A solar panel can cut down on the cost of heating your water.

The *a* form is used before words and abbreviations that begin with a consonant, eg *a monkey*, *a garden gnome*, *a hotel*, *a hot tip*, *a historical novel*, *a youngish man*, *a FIFA ruling*, *a G8 summit*, *a BSc*.

You also use *a* before words and abbreviations that begin with a vowel but are pronounced as though they begin with a consonant, eg *a European*, *a uniformed policeman*, *a UN delegate*, *a unique find*.

You use *an* before words and abbreviations that begin with a vowel, eg *an apple*, *an envelope*, *an Eastern custom*, *an infant*, *an interesting lecture*, *an outboard motor*, *an undertaker*, *an e-mail*, *an AGM*.

You also use *an* before words and abbreviations that begin with a consonant but are pronounced as though they begin with a vowel, eg *an hour*, *an honourable man*, *an FDA report*, *an HND*, *an LP*, *an MEP*, *an NBC broadcast*, *an X-rated movie*.

> **i**
>
> Some speakers prefer to use **an** instead of **a** before certain words beginning with **h**, where the norm is **a**. When **an** is used before such words, the **h** is silent, eg **an hotel**, **an habitual thief**, **an hereditary peerage**, **an historic agreement**. Americans say **an herb**, where again the **h** is silent.

You use *a* or *an* before a singular count noun. You also use it before the count use of a noun that is both count and uncount (see pages 22–4). So for example you can say:

Use a margarine that is low in cholesterol.

She was wearing a fragrant French perfume.

He did me a great injustice.

It's so hot I think I'll have a lemonade rather than a coffee.

You can also use the indefinite article with an uncount noun when it is preceded by an adjective, or followed by a prepositional phrase or relative clause that gives more information about the noun:

a great sadness

an enormous pride

a fear of the future

a knowledge of the theory

an intelligence that everyone respected

a friendliness that I warmed to

The indefinite article is not used before people's names or place names except when you are mentioning someone or something you do not know, or when there are or may be two or more people or places with the same name:

There's a Peter Jones on the phone for you. He didn't say what he was calling about.

There's also a Birmingham in Alabama. Which one do you mean?

Other general determiners

Other general determiners are used to indicate how much of something or how many people or things you mean. They are listed at the beginning of this section.

DETERMINERS

- *Some* and *any* are used before plural count nouns and uncount nouns. *Some* indicates that there is a quantity of something or that there are a number of things or people, where no precise number is given. *Any* is used when you are referring to a quantity of something that may or may not exist. *Any* is used in negative statements to say that something does not exist. Both are used in questions, but *some* generally expects a positive answer while *any* leaves the question open:

  Add some *black pepper to the sauce.*

  There aren't any *eggs left.*

  Would you like some *fudge?*

  Are there any *questions?*

- *A few* and *few* are used before plural count nouns, and *a little* and *little* are used before uncount nouns. *A few* and *a little* indicate that you are referring to a small quantity, while *few* and *little* are used to emphasize how small the quantity is. Compare:

  I have a few *good friends.*

  I have few *good friends.*

  He's had a little *success.*

  He's had little *success.*

- *Fewer* and *fewest* may be used to indicate graded amounts on a scale. They are used before plural count nouns. *Less* and *least* have the same function and are used before uncount nouns:

  Fewer *people are using public transport.*

  Which system is likely to give the fewest *problems?*

  People should eat less *fat.*

I think I do the least work of anyone in the office.

Usage

Less is sometimes used before plural nouns:

There are less jobs available now.

Less people are travelling by train.

Many people think this is wrong, and that **fewer** should be used instead.

- *Another* and *other* are used to refer to similar or additional things or people. *Another* is used before singular count nouns, and *other* before plural count nouns:

   Another day passed.

   She's not like other people.

- *All* is used before plural count nouns and uncount nouns. It is used to include every person or thing of a particular kind:

   All men aren't like him, you know.

   All traffic was at a standstill.

- *Both* is used before plural count nouns to indicate that two people or things are involved in a situation or action. *Either* is used before a singular count noun or an uncount noun when a choice is being presented between two alternatives, and *neither* is used to exclude both of the people or things mentioned:

   Both rooms are occupied.

   It could have gone either way.

Neither side was prepared to back down.

- *Enough* is used to indicate that there is as much of something as is needed. It is used before plural count nouns and uncount nouns:

    There aren't enough tents for everyone.

    Is there enough room in the back?

- *Much*, *many* and *several* indicate that there is a lot of something or a large number of people or things. *Much* is used before uncount nouns and *many* and *several* are used before plural count nouns. The comparative form is *more*, and *most* indicates a majority of people or things:

    You aren't having much luck, are you?

    There weren't many people there.

    I lived there for several years.

    More children should learn foreign languages.

    Most people would agree with me, I'm sure.

- *No* is used before singular or plural count nouns and uncount nouns:

    There are no dry towels in the bathroom.

    There is no reason to doubt her.

    They meant no harm.

- *Each* is used when referring to individual members of a group made up of two or more people or things. *Every* is used when making a general statement about all the members of a group. *Each* and *every* are used before singular count nouns, or before 'one':

Each man will be issued with ten rounds of ammunition.

She was carrying two heavy bags in each hand.

As the boys filed past each one gave his name to the teacher.

Nearly every family will be affected by the factory closures.

There were so many letters it was impossible to reply to every one.

Exclamative determiners

The exclamative determiners *what* and *such* are used in exclamations that express surprise, astonishment, admiration, wonder etc:

What nonsense!

What rubbish they write in the newspapers!

Such skill!

What big ears you've got, grandma!

Interrogative determiners

The interrogative determiners are *which*, *what* and *whose*. They are used before count nouns in the singular or plural:

What make of car do you drive?

What ingredients do we need to make moussaka?

With what type of weapon was he murdered?

Which kind do you prefer?

Which hairdresser do you go to?

By which gate did you enter?

Whose bag is this?

Whose books are those?

With whose permission did you leave?

Note that these words are also interrogative pronouns.

Pre-determiners

These come before another determiner. The general determiners *all*, *both* and *many* are also pre-determiners. *All* and *both* can be used before a specific determiner, and *many* can be used before the indefinite article:

> *All the trees were in blossom.*
>
> *All my clothes need washing.*
>
> *Both these arguments are convincing.*
>
> *I saw him many a time.*

Such and *what* are exclamatives that may also function as pre-determiners. *What* can be used before the definite or indefinite article, and *such* can be used before the indefinite article:

> *What a mess!*
>
> *Oh, what the hell!*
>
> *She's such a liar!*

Double, *half*, *quarter* and *twice* are always pre-determiners. They are used before a specific determiner:

> *I won double my money.*
>
> *I could do it in half the time.*
>
> *It should cost quarter the price.*
>
> *She's got twice the energy of a young woman.*

Quite and *rather* are always pre-determiners, and are used before the indefinite article:

> *I had* quite *a nice time.*
>
> *He's* quite *a success.*
>
> *It's* rather *a nice day.*
>
> *It's* rather *a pity.*

Post-determiners

These are words such as *usual* and *same*, which are used after determiners and before any other adjectives. They are also known as **specifying adjectives**. (For examples, see page 91.)

Order of determiners

More than one determiner can be used in a noun group. A pre-determiner comes before all other determiners, followed by a specific determiner, followed by a general determiner:

> *He had to buy presents for* all his many *relatives.*

Quantifiers

Most of the general determiners are also quantifiers, that is, they can be followed by *of*. The exceptions are the indefinite article, *every*, *fewest*, *least*, *no* and *other*. These examples show the quantifier use of the general determiners:

> *A few* of them attended the meeting.*
>
> *He was talking to* all *of them.*
>
> *There was nothing that* any *of us can do.*
>
> *Both* of them were rescued.*
>
> *I can't stand* either *of those blue cheeses.*

Few of them passed the test.

Little of the money was invested.

Many of these people don't have televisions.

Several of the demonstrators were arrested.

Some of the holidaymakers were delayed for nine hours.

Checklist

Determiners are used before nouns to specify them or to indicate whether they are of a particular type.

1. **Specific determiners**
   - are used to refer to a particular person or thing

2. **Definite article:** *the*
   - are used before uncount nouns and singular and plural count nouns
   - are used when referring to something or someone for a second time or when the hearer is expected to know which person or thing you mean
   - are used before a singular count noun to refer to an entire class or species, eg *The piranha is a predator*
   - are used before an adjective to give a collective label to people, eg *the unemployed*
   - are used before some place names and in names of buildings etc, eg *the Netherlands*

3. **Demonstrative determiners:** *this*, *that*, *these* **and** *those*
   - have singular forms (*this* and *that*) and plural forms (*these* and *those*)
   - come before a noun
   - can also function as pronouns

4. Possessive determiners
- refer to something belonging to or connected with somebody or something, eg *his*, *their*
- can be singular or plural and can be masculine, feminine or neuter
- can be followed by 'own' for emphasis, eg *That's his own business*

5. General determiners
- are used when referring to someone or something for the first time, or in general terms, eg *any*, *most*

6. Indefinite article: *a* and *an*
- are used before a count noun to refer to people or things in a general way or for the first time
- takes the form *a* or *an* depending on the following word
- can be used before people's names or place names if they are unknown or when there is more than one of them, eg *There's a̲ Mrs Smith here to see you*

7. Exclamative determiners: *what* and *such*
- express surprise, astonishment, disbelief etc, eg *S̲u̲c̲h̲ a racket!*
- can function as pre-determiners, eg *W̲h̲a̲t̲ a day!*

8. Interrogative determiners: *which*, *what* and *whose*
- are used before count nouns in the singular or plural

9. Pre-determiners
- are used before other determiners, eg *double*, *quite*, *rather*, *such*

10. Post-determiners
- are used after determiners and before any other adjectives, eg *the s̲a̲m̲e̲ old faces*

11. Order of determiners
- usually pre-determiner ▶ specific determiner ▶ general determiner

12. Quantifiers
- are general determiners used to talk about the number or amount of people or things, eg *all*, *every*

Grammar in practice

A Underline the determiners in the following sentences. The number in brackets tells you how many there are:

1 *When we'd saved a little money, after the first few years, we bought the land for this house. (5)*

2 *We talked about my family and hers, our friends and what they were doing. (2)*

3 *I had enough time for a cup of tea and another slice of toast. (3)*

4 *He had developed a habit of starting his answer to any question with the words 'Well, no … yes.' (4)*

5 *I took several lungfuls of the clean, sweet air. (2)*

6 *Cook the meat until browned on both sides. (2)*

7 *There are some details that require much thought. (2)*

8 *She knew all the answers to our questions. (3)*

9 *In those days, a ten-minute walk would get you out of the city and into the wilds. (4)*

10 *Within a few months the rector died, and Manning stepped into his shoes. (3)*

B Fill in the gaps in the following sentences using *a few*, *few*, *a little* or *little*:

1 *She's called you* .... *times today.*

2 *I had too much worry, and too* .... *sleep.*

3 *Slice the meat and pour* .... *sauce over it.*

4 *Unfortunately there was* .... *media coverage of this exciting event.*

5 *We met on one of your* .... *trips to the library.*

6 *Thicken the mixture with flour and* .... *water.*

7 *There was never any vandalism and* .... *cigarette butts were dropped on the floor.*

8 *The city was almost deserted and* .... *people passed us in the street.*

9 *I had* .... *choice but to agree.*

10 *We managed to sleep for* .... *hours.*

Prepositions and prepositional phrases

Prepositions are a closed class, though there are more of them than is typical of closed classes. They allow us to talk about place, time, and other situations. Prepositions may be single words, eg *against*, *by*, *with*, *from*. They may be *-ing* words, eg *concerning*, *considering*, *regarding*. Prepositions may also be combinations of two or more words, eg *according to*, *except for*, *in spite of*.

A preposition is normally followed by a noun group, forming a **prepositional phrase**. The noun group after the preposition is sometimes called a **prepositional object**. Prepositional phrases may form part of a noun group:

> The man *on my left* is my neighbour.

Or they may function like adverbs, when they are used as the **adjunct** in a clause:

> *Off the motorway,* you'll discover a network of minor roads.

For more information on the use of prepositional phrases as adjuncts, see page 102.

Some meanings of prepositions

Prepositions express a wide variety of different meanings. The two most important ones are place and time.

Place, position and movement

The following prepositions indicate where someone or something is, or where they are going:

above	at	beyond	inside	opposite	to
across	behind	by	into	out of	towards
along	below	down	near	outside	under
among	beneath	from	off	over	under- neath
around	beside	in	on	past	up
away from	between	in front of	onto	through	

Here are some examples:

> *Our house is near the shops.*

> *He said he'd meet me outside the cinema.*

> *Pass those papers to me, would you?*

> *I stayed in my room all day.*

> *He jumped onto the train just as it was leaving the station.*

> *My road is past the traffic lights.*

> *He had to climb through the window.*

> *You'll find it under that pile of books.*

> *I just arrived from the station.*

> *In front of the house there's a large apple tree.*

Time

The following prepositions indicate when something happened or how long it lasted for:

PREPOSITIONS AND PREPOSITIONAL PHRASES

about	at	during	on	until
after	before	for	since	
around	by	in	till	

Here are some examples:

> *We arrived at noon.*
>
> *It happened in January.*
>
> *It was the calm before the storm.*
>
> *You can't lie in bed for the whole weekend.*
>
> *Do you want to go for a drink after work?*
>
> *I'll see you on Tuesday.*
>
> *He left about ten o'clock.*
>
> *It's been raining since daybreak.*
>
> *I'll be staying until Saturday.*
>
> *I don't often sleep during the day.*

Other meanings

Not all prepositions indicate place or time. Others indicate a variety of relationships between people, things and situations. The following examples illustrate some of these relationships:

> *She had strong feelings of jealousy.*
>
> *He stepped down as chairman.*
>
> *They are going to vote on it.*
>
> *I grieved for everything I had lost.*
>
> *He was complaining about the weather.*
>
> *She's campaigning against arranged marriages.*
>
> *His life centres around his family.*
>
> *Jack arrived with his partner.*

The price works out at 70 pence a tin.

The government lost by one vote.

She stands out from the crowd.

John deals in antiques.

Don't go without me.

There are ten of us including me.

We are looking for information regarding his disappear-ance.

Everyone arrived on time except for Martin.

Certain verbs are always followed by a particular preposition, eg accuse someone *of*, believe *in*, congratulate someone *on*, deprive someone *of*, distinguish *between*, refrain *from*. These are not considered to be phrasal verbs because they are not idiomatic in meaning.

Prepositions in phrasal verbs

Like adverbs, prepositions often combine with verbs to form phrasal verbs. When prepositions are used in phrasal verbs they are known as **particles**:

I had to look after the kids all day.

She came across a letter from her grandmother.

He sailed through his maths exam.

My friends stuck by me through thick and thin.

Jane takes after her mother.

Bullies pick on younger children.

The police plan to look into the matter.

Some phrasal verbs have two particles, an adverb followed by a preposition:

I don't have to put up with all this hassle, you know.

I look forward to hearing from you.

For more information about phrasal verbs, see pages 47–8.

Position of prepositions

Usually a preposition comes before a noun group to form a prepositional phrase. In some sentence structures, however, the preposition can be separated from its object. This happens in:

- questions and reported questions:

  Who are you writing to?

  Which drawer did you get these files out of?

  She asked what we were talking about.

- relative clauses:

  I found the address I was looking for.

  Those are the stairs that you should have gone up.

  She's the person I feel sorry for in all this mess.

- passive voice:

  I don't like being made a fool of.

  The tests are paid for by the patient.

  The proposals are still being worked on.

- to-infinitive constructions:

  She's very easy to talk to.

  The screw is hard to get at.

You need a bag to put your clothes in.

- comparisons:

  This was more than I had bargained for.

  Two children are as many as I can cope with.

  We have as much help as we ask for.

Prepositions and adverbs

Many prepositions are also adverbs. The most frequent ones are:
about, *above*, *across*, *after*, *against*, *along*, *around*, *before*, *behind*, *below*, *beneath*, *beside*, *between*, *beyond*, *by*, *down*, *in*, *inside*, *near*, *off*, *on*, *opposite*, *outside*, *over*, *past*, *since*, *through*, *under*, *up*, *with*, *without*.

Checklist

1. **Prepositions**
   - may be single words (eg *against*), -ing words (eg *concerning*) or combinations of two or more words (eg *except for*)
   - are normally followed by a noun group to form a prepositional phrase, eg *He sailed <u>across the sea</u>*
   - may function like adverbs when they are used as the adjunct in a clause, eg *He bought a cake <u>in the bakery</u>*

2. **Place, position and movement**
   - are indicated by prepositions such as *beyond*, *behind*, *off*, *over*

3. **Time and duration**
   - are indicated by prepositions such as *around*, *until*, *since*

4. **Other meanings indicated by prepositions**
   - include a variety of relationships between people, things and situations, eg *He protested <u>against</u> the war*

5. **Verbs and prepositions**
- often combine in fixed ways, eg *refrain from*, *deprive of*

6. **Phrasal verbs**
- are formed by combining prepositions (known as particles) and verbs to create an idiomatic meaning, eg *take after*, *pack in*, *get over*
- can consist of two particles, eg *put up with*

7. **Position of prepositions**
- is usually before a noun group, forming a prepositional phrase, eg *He found shade under the big oak tree*.

8. **Preposition can be separated from its object**
- in questions and reported questions, eg *What are you looking for?*
- in relative clauses, eg *This is the book I told you about*
- in the passive voice, eg *The notes were written by the doctor*
- in *to*-infinitive constructions, eg *The machine was difficult to turn on*
- in comparisons, eg *This was less than I had asked for*

9. **Prepositions and adverbs**
- are often the same, eg *about*, *near*, *outside*, *since*

Grammar in practice

A Use the prepositions below to fill in the gaps in the following sentences:

beyond	opposite	during	for	about
including	without	in	against	at

1 *It's hard to get a job .... any qualifications.*

2 *What have you been doing out .... this weather?*

3 *The building of new houses extends far .... the city limits.*

4 *We need to protect ourselves .... the threat of nuclear war.*

5 *Several families lost their homes .... the fighting.*

6 *The train station is .... the Grand Victoria Hotel.*

7 *He had all the tools he needed, ... a circular saw.*

8 *Can the desired improvements be achieved .... less cost?*

9 *I just want to lie down .... a while.*

10 *There is not much .... the place to attract tourists.*

B Fill in the gaps in the following sentences using *at, in* or *on*:

1 *I live .... Bristol, ... Beech Road.*

2 *The village is .... the road to Kidderminster.*

3 *He punched him .... the eye and knocked him over.*

4 *Jo was wild .... school, and dropped out .... the age of 16.*

5 *She worked .... a hotel during the school holidays.*

C The following sentences all contain phrasal verbs, with the preposition omitted. Fill in the gaps with an appropriate preposition:

1 *We need to look .... the possibilities of wind-generated electricity.*

2 *What lies .... such crimes is pure and simple greed.*

3 *These old fireplaces are hard to come ....*

4 *I have not entered .... any financial agreements.*

5 *He was living .... £600 a month.*

Conjunctions

This chapter deals with the words whose function is to link words, groups and clauses together. These linking words are called conjunctions. They are a closed class.

There are two types of conjunction: **co-ordinating conjunctions** and **subordinating conjunctions**.

Co-ordinating conjunctions

Co-ordinating conjunctions link grammatically independent elements of equal weight or importance (words, groups or clauses). The main co-ordinating conjunctions are *and*, *but*, *yet*, *or* and *nor*. Each of these indicates what kind of link is being made: *and* introduces an addition, *but* and *yet* signal some kind of contrast, and *or* and *nor* signal positive and negative alternatives. *So* and *then* are also co-ordinating conjunctions when the elements being linked are clauses.

- In the examples below, conjunctions link words within a single group or prepositional phrase:

    a black and white striped shirt

    an old but useful rucksack

    A child's early education is important in shaping his or her life.

    He was a strict yet fair leader.

    She walked to and from school.

- In the examples below, conjunctions link two groups or prepositional phrases:

He's an electrician and a skilled carpenter.
[noun groups]

They were laughing and enjoying themselves.
[verb groups]

Jill didn't come, nor did John.
[verb groups]

She was talented and very experienced.
[adjective groups]

We were exhausted but rather pleased with our achievement.
[adjective groups]

The work was simple yet very tiring.
[adjective groups]

He was working slowly but quite carefully.
[adverb groups]

We walked along the road and up the hill.
[prepositional phrases]

- In the examples below, conjunctions link two clauses. You can also use *so* (in the sense of *also*) or *then* as co-ordinating conjunctions when you are linking clauses. *So* and *then* are often used after *and*.

  Theresa wants to be a doctor and Roy wants to be an astronaut.

  I wanted to leave but I felt it was too early.

  I don't eat much, yet I am a size 16.

  You must talk to him about it, or I will.

  Julie has changed recently, and so has her husband.

If you are joining two or more words, groups or clauses, there is usually only one conjunction, which appears before the final element. Some people use commas between the penultimate and the last element, and some do not:

> *She speaks French, Italian,* and *Spanish.*
>
> *Would you like eggs, bacon* or *kippers for breakfast?*

You often use *either ... or* or *neither ... nor* respectively between the two elements you are joining.

> *He's* either *lying,* or *hiding something.*
>
> *I am* neither *a liar* nor *a thief.*

Two or more groups or clauses may be co-ordinated without any linking conjunction:

> *Friends, Romans, countrymen, lend me your ears*
>
> *Gently, lovingly, she stroked his cheek.*

Often when you link two groups, clauses etc, you can omit certain words from the second one to avoid repetition:

> *I gazed at the hazy blue of the sea* and *sky.*
>
> *She might be shopping* or *collecting the children from school.*

In the first sentence, you do not need to say 'and *the* sky', and in the second you do not need to say 'or *she might be* collecting the children from school'. This is known as **ellipsis** (see also page 174).

Subordinating conjunctions

Subordinating conjunctions introduce subordinate clauses: that is, they come at the beginning of a subordinate clause and link it with the main clause. They are not used to link words, groups or prepositional phrases. The difference between clauses linked by co-ordinating conjunctions and those linked by subordinating conjunctions is that co-ordinated clauses are equally important, whereas subordinate clauses are dependent on a main clause.

Some of the subordinating conjunctions are *after*, *although*, *as*, *because*, *if*, *until*, *which*. For more information on the kinds of clauses that these introduce, see pages 176–81.

Checklist

Conjunctions link words, groups and clauses together.

1. Co-ordinating conjunctions
- link words, groups or clauses of equal weight or importance
- are used to signify addition (eg *and*), signal a contrast (eg *but*, *yet*) or indicate alternatives (eg *or*, *nor*)
- can be paired, eg *He liked both going to the opera and walking in the park*

2. Ellipsis
- occurs when certain words are omitted from the second group or clause linked by a co-ordinating conjunction, eg *The police arrived and (the police) arrested the protesters*

3. Subordinating conjunctions
- introduce subordinate clauses, which are dependent on the main clause, eg *I will be annoyed if you are late*
- are not used to link words, groups or prepositional phrases

Grammar in practice

Identify the co-ordinating conjunctions in the following sentences and say which elements they are linking. Also say whether there has been any ellipsis, that is, whether some elements have been dropped after the first group or clause:

1 *She said yes, then she said no, then yes again.*

2 *They can sit either on the benches or on the grass.*

3 *She's only twelve but smart as a whip.*

4 *Sid played with his children, wrestling with them or playing hide-and-seek.*

5 *He spent the summer climbing in North Wales, then volunteered for the Marines.*

6 *He was leaving for Rome the next day and had a great deal to do.*

7 *Don't eat fatty foods or red meat.*

8 *Fold all the ingredients together quickly, yet very carefully.*

9 *He looked at her with an amused but approving smile.*

10 *He wanted grandchildren, yet neither his son nor his daughter had obliged so far.*

11 *Patrick and Jason were polite to each other, but they were not friends.*

12 *She hadn't gone swimming or been to the gym in the last week or two.*

13 *He was highly motivated, competent and independent.*

14 *I was interested in reading it, and so was my wife.*

15 *People say sheep are stupid but they're not.*

Numbers

There are three main types of number: **cardinal numbers**, **ordinal numbers** and **fractions**.

Cardinal numbers

Cardinal numbers, eg *one*, *two*, *fourteen*, *twenty-six* are used to indicate a quantity. They may be written out as words, eg *zero*, *three*, *ten*, *ninety-nine*, *a thousand*, or using the digits from *0* to *9*, eg *7*, *29*, *700*, *20,000*. In books, newspapers etc, the usual practice is to spell out the lower numbers and to use digits for the higher numbers. In this book, we use words for the numbers *one* to *twelve*, and digits for numbers from twelve onwards, eg *13*, *72*. Note that when numbers from 21 to 99 are written out, they are written with a hyphen, eg *fifty-eight*, *ninety-nine*. This does not apply to multiples of ten, eg *ten*, *fifty*, *seventy*.

The number *one* is used with a singular count noun, eg *one cow*, and all the other cardinal numbers are used with plural count nouns, eg *nine crocodiles*. However, when you are mentioning a sum of money, a distance etc, you use a singular verb:

> *Ten pounds is a lot to pay for a ticket.*
>
> *Nine miles is quite a long way to walk.*

Words used as alternative terms for *zero* are also considered to be cardinal numbers, eg *nought*, *nil*, *love*, *nothing*. The same goes for other quantities, eg *a dozen* (twelve) and *a score* (20).

Cardinal numbers can be plural in form:

> *It will cost thousands of dollars.*

It will cost many millions.

Scores of people were left without electricity.

He's in his fifties.

Note that in these examples, the number is not exact: *scores of people* just means 'a large number of people'. *Dozens, hundreds, thousands* and *millions* are also used to mean 'a large number':

I've dozens of friends.

I've told you that hundreds of times.

There were thousands of people there.

Note too that when cardinal numbers are used to mean 'a large number', they function as quantifiers; that is, they are followed by *of* and then a noun.

When you use a determiner and a number in front of a noun, the determiner comes before the number. When the noun group contains an adjective, the number comes before the adjective:

the four men

All four children came to her party.

my two lovely daughters

Cardinal numbers can function as nouns:

Have you got a five in these shoes?

Six tens are sixty.

She was a sixteen before she went on a diet; now she's a twelve.

The first eleven won the match.

The temperature was in the eighties that day.

Those zeros look like eights.

They can also function as pronouns:

We have two children and they have three.

They caught one boy but the other two ran off.

Note that singular forms of the cardinal numbers *hundred*, *thousand*, *million* and *billion* cannot stand alone. They are always preceded by an article or another cardinal number. Note too that they are used in the singular after a cardinal number:

a million dollars

ten thousand men

When can you give me the hundred pounds you owe me?

Words like *about*, *nearly*, *over*, *under*, *some*, *almost*, *less than*, *more than* and *fewer than* are used with numbers to indicate approximate quantities.

He's nearly thirty.

There were more than a hundred people there.

Ordinal numbers

The ordinal numbers, eg *fourth* and *hundredth*, indicate the position of someone or something in an order or sequence. They may be written out as words, eg *first*, *second*, *fifth*, *seventeenth*, *thirtieth*, or as digits followed by letters, eg *1st*, *2nd*, *3rd*, *4th*. Most ordinal numbers (except *first*, *second* and *third*) are formed by adding *-th* to the corresponding cardinal number. When the *-th* ending is added to certain cardinals, the ending of the cardinal number changes, eg *fifth*, *twelfth*, *twentieth*, or a letter is dropped, eg *eighth*, *ninth*.

Ordinal numbers are usually preceded by a determiner:

> the *third* Duke
>
> It's her *first* day at school.
>
> She asked for a *second* helping.
>
> Today is my *sixteenth* birthday.
>
> the *30th* of October

Certain other words have the same grammatical function as ordinal numbers, eg *next*, *last*, *additional*, *further*, *following*, *preceding*, *latter*, *previous*, *subsequent*. These are sometimes called **post-determiners** (see page 145), in that they come after a determiner and before other adjectives.

Ordinals (and post-determiners) may be used in the same noun group as a cardinal number:

> The *first* three lottery numbers are 13, 17 and 21.
>
> The *next* ten days will be crucial.

Ordinal numbers can function as pronouns:

> We're going on holiday on the *fifth*.
>
> I got the first prize and he got the *second*.

They can also function as adverbs:

> He came in *ninth*.
>
> I got there *first*.

They can also function as quantifiers:

> This is the *third* of my four daughters.
>
> I read the *second* of his three novels.

Fractions

A fraction is a quantity that is less than one or less than a whole, eg *a half*, *a quarter*, *three-fifths*. Fractions may be written out as words or as figures, one above the other and separated by a horizontal line, eg $^1/_2$, $^3/_4$, $^5/_6$.

When a fraction represents only one part, it may be written out preceded by *one* or *a*:

> *one half* or *a half*
>
> *one fifth* or *a fifth*

When you are talking about halves or quarters, there is a choice of forms, eg *half a kilo of oranges*, *a quarter of a kilo of oranges*, or *a half kilo of oranges*. The last of these is preferred in American English.

Fractions can function as nouns:

> *Two quarters make a half.*
>
> *What do you get when you add one third and one sixteenth?*

Fractions can also function as quantifiers:

> *three-quarters of the population*
>
> *ten thousandths of a second*

They can also function as pronouns:

> *Half of the students are French.*
>
> *Only a quarter attended the meeting.*

Cardinal numbers and fractions are often combined:

> *two* and a *half* pounds
>
> *three* and *three-quarter* litres

Checklist

1. Cardinal numbers

- are used to indicate a quantity
- can be written as words or digits
- can also take forms such as *a dozen*, *nought*, *zero*
- function as quantifiers when they are used to mean 'a large number', eg *dozens of books*
- can function as nouns and pronouns

2. Ordinal numbers

- indicate the position of someone or something in an order or sequence, eg *first*, *second*
- can be written as words or digits
- are usually formed by adding *-th* to the cardinal numbers, and sometimes changing the ending of the cardinal number eg *fifth*, *ninth*
- are usually preceded by a determiner, eg <u>*the*</u> *second son*
- can function as pronouns, adverbs or quantifiers

3. Post-determiners

- have the same grammatical function as ordinal numbers, eg *next*, *following*
- come after a determiner and before other adjectives, eg *The <u>following</u> five hours dragged by*

4. Fractions

- are quantities less than one or less than a whole, eg *a half*, *a third*
- can function as nouns, quantifiers and pronouns

5. Cardinal numbers and fractions
- are often combined, eg *three and a half kilos*

Grammar in practice

A State whether the numbers in the following sentences are cardinal numbers, ordinal numbers or fractions:

1 *Its diameter is approximately one-fifth of its distance from the sun.*

2 *Spoon half the mixture into a shallow dish.*

3 *She had nine grandchildren.*

4 *She'd reached the age of seven.*

5 *Her mother is the seventh child of a seventh child and has second sight.*

6 *The comet came within one-tenth of Earth's distance from the sun.*

7 *He finished fifth in the race.*

8 *Pre-heat the oven to 170 degrees.*

9 *We paid less than a third of the market value of the property.*

10 *Roast until three-quarters cooked, then remove from the oven.*

B Put the numbers, determiners and adjectives in the following noun groups into the correct order:

    1 *two these considerations primary*

    2 *more six him like*

    3 *years those three first*

    4 *billion dollars four*

    5 *miles twelve another*

Clauses and sentences

A **sentence** is a unit that begins with a capital letter and ends with a full stop, a question mark or an exclamation mark. A sentence may consist of one or more clauses. A clause is a unit of language that consists of a predicate (or verb) and usually a subject. It may also contain a direct object, an indirect object, a complement, an object complement and one or more adjuncts. See pages 6–11 for further information about the constituents of a clause.

Types of sentence

Sentences may be described according to how many clauses or what kind of clause they contain. By this criterion there are three types of sentence:

Simple sentence

A simple sentence is one that consists of only one clause. It usually contains a finite verb, that is, a verb that shows tense, aspect, number and person:

> *Stop!*
>
> *Their plane has landed.*
>
> *The sun rises in the east.*
>
> *My son ran away from school.*
>
> *He is very good-looking.*
>
> *Harry had given me the money by mistake.*

Compound sentence

A compound sentence is one in which there are two or more main clauses, usually linked by co-ordinating conjunctions. The co-ordinated clauses are of equal importance:

> *Liz peeled the potatoes and Ginny prepared the vegetables.*
>
> *I'd like to leave now, but I don't want to seem rude.*
>
> *I try to get up early, yet I always seem to be late for work.*
>
> *I'm not sure whether I was pushed over or whether I just fell.*
>
> *Just as Joe has changed, so has his wife.*
>
> *Add the onion and then simmer for ten minutes.*

The next examples have three co-ordinated clauses. Note that there does not need to be a co-ordinating conjunction between the first two:

> *Your calls will be answered more quickly, the lines will be clearer and there will be fewer faults.*
>
> *She laughed, then turned round and left the room.*

The clauses in compound sentences may be linked by a semi-colon rather than a co-ordinating conjunction:

> *Jeff is following in his father's footsteps; he is training to be a vet.*

A pronoun is often used in the second clause to avoid repeating the subject:

> *Hannah was born in England but she grew up in India.*

When the subject is the same in each clause of a compound sentence, the subject is often dropped from the second clause. This is known as **ellipsis**:

> *Jeff followed in his father's footsteps and became a vet.*
> [*he* has been dropped]

> *She was brought up in Nigeria and has devoted her life to drama.*
> [*she* has been dropped]

The main verb or both the verb and the object can also be dropped:

> *Add the oil and then the garlic.*
> [*add* has been dropped]

> *He said he'd help me but he didn't.*
> [*help me* has been dropped]

Complex sentence

A complex sentence is one in which there is a main clause and two or more **subordinate clauses**. The main clause is grammatically independent and the subordinate clauses are dependent on it. The main and subordinate clauses are linked by a subordinating conjunction. In the following examples, the subordinate clauses are highlighted:

> *Your application wasn't successful because you don't have the appropriate qualifications.*

> *She might catch the last bus if she leaves now.*

> *When there is no moon, we can move around without being seen.*

Note that the subordinate clause can come before or after the main clause.

A pronoun is often used in a subordinate clause to avoid repeating the subject. This can happen even when the subordinate clause comes first:

> Patricia turned very pale *when she saw the blood*.
>
> *When she saw the blood*, Patricia turned very pale.

Sometimes there are more than two subordinate clauses; the first is dependent on the main clause and the second is dependent on the first. The first subordinate clause is highlighted and the second is underlined.

> It won't be surprising *if people complain* <u>*if they don't punish him*</u>.
>
> I don't mind *if you leave* <u>*as soon as you've finished*</u>.

Non-finite clauses

Some subordinate clauses are non-finite, that is, they contain verb groups that are not marked for tense and aspect, and do not show number or person. The non-finite forms are the *to*-infinitive, the *-ing* form (the present participle) or the *-ed* form (the past participle):

> *To make a good impression*, you should always be polite and respectful.
>
> *Weather permitting*, we will start at six pm.
>
> She had a puncture *while driving to work*.
>
> *Angered by the decision to go to war*, she took part in a protest march.

For more examples of non-finite clauses, see the types of subordinate clause below.

Compound sentences may also include main and subordinate clauses. The subordinate clauses are in italics:

I would if I could, but I can't.

Angus feeds the calves and Liam mucks out the horses before they come in for breakfast.

When the bell rang, the children piled out into the play-ground and the teachers retired to the staff room.

You can use ellipsis in a subordinate clause:

They can't translate the document, whereas we can.
[*translate the document* has been dropped]

Don't finish it if you don't want to.
[*finish it* has been dropped]

Types of subordinate clause

The main types of subordinate clause are **adverbial clauses** and **relative clauses**. We are not dealing with **noun clauses** here, because they are not subordinate; instead they function as the subject or object of a verb (see page 7).

Adverbial clause

There are nine types of adverbial clause:

- **Purpose clauses** answer the question 'What for?' and are linked to the main clause by the subordinating conjunctions *in order that*, *in order to*, *so*, *so that* and *so as to*. This type of clause can come before or after the main clause:

    I put the plant on the windowsill so that it would get more light.

    In order that these matters can be dealt with quickly, parliament is being recalled a week early.

Some purpose clauses are non-finite:

They bought some of his land in order to extend their farm.

I didn't tell her the truth, so as not to alarm her.

Some non-finite purpose clauses have no subordinating conjunction, but begin with a *to*-infinitive instead:

We huddled together to keep warm.

- **Result clauses** express a result or a consequence, and are usually linked to the main clause by the subordinating conjunctions *so* and *so that*. (Note that *so that* can also be used in purpose clauses with a different meaning.) This type of clause comes after the main clause:

I was an only child, so I had no experience of large families.

Come to my room so that I can tell you all about my trip to New York.

You can also use *so* or *such* and *that* in a structure to say that a result happens because something has a lot of a particular quality:

The snow was falling so thick and fast that they had to pull in to a lay-by.

She speaks so quickly that few people understand her.

My dog is such a wonderful companion that I would be lost without him.

- **Reason clauses** answer the question 'Why?' and are linked to the main clause by the subordinating conjunctions *as*, *because*, *in case* and *since*. This type of clause can come before or after the main clause:

I don't have time to see you as I have too much work to do.

She stopped the car because it was snowing very heavily.

I've brought the keys in case you want to see inside.

Since you ask, I'll tell you what I know.

- **Concessive clauses** are clauses that contrast with the main clause in some way, or make something seem surprising. They are linked to the main clause by the subordinating conjunctions *although*, *despite*, *even if*, *even though*, *except that*, *in spite of*, *much as*, *not that*, *though*, *whereas*, *while* and *whilst*. This type of clause can come before or after the main clause:

    I can remember his departure although I was only six at the time.

    They gave her the part in spite of the fact that she had never acted before.

    Things are going to be different from now on, even if you don't realize it yet.

    Much as I enjoyed the film, I'm not going with you to see it again.

Some concessive clauses are non-finite:

    Though wanting to see her very much, he refused to try to make contact.

    Although originally written in Gaelic, his poems have been translated into several languages.

- **Clauses of manner** answer the question 'How?' and are linked to the main clause by the subordinating conjunctions *as*, *as if*, *as though*, *just as*, *like*, and *the way (that)*. This type of clause comes after the main clause:

> *Now secure the tent flap with a couple of pegs as I showed you.*

> *He treats me as though I'm a child.*

> *I don't understand why he lies like he does.*

> *He's earning his living the same way his father and grandfather did.*

> *I felt dazed, as if I'd been hit on the head.*

Some clauses of manner are non-finite:

> *He looked at her as though puzzled.*

- **Clauses of comparison** are used to compare things and people, and are linked to the main clause using the constructions *as ... as*, *so ... as*, *more ... than* and *less ... than*. This type of clause comes after the main clause, though the first of the pairs of words are in the main clause:

> *It's as hot today as it was yesterday.*

> *The problem is more serious than it was before.*

- **Conditional clauses** are used to talk about a possible situation. They are linked to the main clause by the subordinating conjunctions *as long as*, *if*, *providing (that)*, *provided that*, *supposing*, *unless* and *whether ... or*. This type of clause can come either before or after the main clause.

Some conditional clauses are used to talk about things that may or may not happen in the future:

> *If you don't do it now, you'll never do it.*

Unless John arrives soon, he'll miss the start of the film.

We'll agree not to take this any further providing you agree to pay for the damage.

I'm leaving whether you want me to or not.

Some are used to talk about hypothetical or imaginary situations:

If I ruled the world, every day would be the first day of spring.

You could be much fitter if you went to the gym more often.

Supposing there was a war, would the government re-introduce conscription?

These clauses are often subjunctive:

If I were you, I'd get rid of the evidence.

Some conditional clauses are used to talk about what might have been, but which didn't happen:

If I had realized you'd be so angry, I wouldn't have said anything.

If she hadn't got married, she might have had a more successful career.

They are also used to make polite requests:

Would you mind if I asked you to move your bags?

Some conditional clauses are non-finite:

He'll only resign if forced to do so.

- **Time clauses** answer the question 'When?' and are linked to the main clause by the subordinating conjunctions *as*, *as soon as*, *after*, *before*, *once*, *since*, *till*, *until*, *when*, *whenever* and *while*. You can also use groups like *each time*, *every time*, *the last time* and *the next time*. This type of clause can come before or after the main clause:

    After he had gone, she sat down and wept.

    Once we've moved the furniture, we can start stripping the walls.

    Wait there until I come.

    My parents adopted me when I was a baby.

    Every time I see you, you've got a new problem.

    My father looked after the children while I was at work.

Some time clauses are non-finite:

    Since moving to the city, I've been mugged twice.

- **Place clauses** answer the question 'Where?' and are linked to the main clause by the subordinating conjunctions *anywhere*, *everywhere*, *where* and *wherever*. This type of clause can come before or after the main clause:

    We tried to find out where the noise was coming from.

    You can park anywhere you like.

    Wherever I go, she follows me.

    Everywhere we go, we see homeless people begging in the streets.

Some place clauses are non-finite:

    You know where to find me.

CLAUSES AND SENTENCES

Relative clause

Relative clauses give further information about something you have just mentioned. They are usually introduced by the relative pronouns *that*, *which*, *who*, *whom*, *whose*, *when* and *where*. For more information on relative pronouns and the grammatical role they play in the clause, see pages 122–4.

There are two main types of relative clause, **defining** and **non-defining**:

Defining relative clauses

Defining relative clauses are not strictly speaking subordinate clauses, because they actually form part of a noun group (see page 15). A defining relative clause is used to explain which person or thing you are talking about. There is no comma between the rest of the noun group and the relative clause. Defining relative clauses are essential to the meaning of the whole sentence and cannot be omitted:

✔ *The one that you want is over there.*

✘ *The one is over there.*

A defining relative clause is used in the construction known in grammar as a **cleft sentence**. A cleft sentence is one that has been split into two clauses so that one part of the sentence is given greater emphasis. Compare the following sentences:

> *Ken must have left the door open.*
>
> *It must have been Ken who left the door open.*
> [cleft sentence]

> *He thought of his family first.*
>
> *It was his family that he thought of first.*
> [cleft sentence]

In both cleft sentences shown above, the part of the sentence being emphasized is contained in the relative clause at the end. The main clause has been given the 'dummy' subject *it*.

Defining relative clauses can be non-finite. When the verb group is passive, both the relative pronoun and the verb *to be* can be omitted:

> *The methods employed by certain officers are giving cause for concern.*

Non-defining relative clauses

Non-defining relative clauses are true subordinate clauses. Non-defining relative clauses add extra information, and the sentence will still make sense if you omit them. There is a comma before the relative clause, and after it, if the main clause continues:

> *The craft shop, which is on Granville Street, sells baskets and pottery made locally.*
>
> *The game, which had been scheduled for Saturday, was played last Tuesday evening.*
>
> *My brother, who I believe you interviewed, has got a job in Hong Kong.*
>
> *The Pearsons, whose house this is, have gone to Australia.*
>
> *In 1990, when he lived in Rome, his daughter fell ill with tuberculosis.*

The relative pronoun **that** cannot be used in non-defining relative clauses.

Checklist

Sentences are units that begin with a capital letter and end with a full stop, question mark or exclamation mark. Sentences can consist of clauses, which consist of a verb and a subject.

1. **Simple sentence**
- consists of one clause
- usually contains a finite verb that shows tense, aspect, number and person

2. **Compound sentence**
- has two or more main clauses, linked by co-ordinating conjunctions or a semicolon
- can also include subordinate clauses

3. **Complex sentence**
- has a main clause and two or more subordinate clauses, linked to the main clause by a subordinating conjunction

4. **Subordinate clause**
- usually contains a pronoun or uses ellipsis to avoid repetition
- can be dependent on either the main clause or on another subordinate clause

5. **Adverbial clause**
- can be one of nine types expressing purpose, result, reason, contrast, manner, comparison, possibility, time or place

6. **Relative clauses**
- give further information
- are usually introduced by relative pronouns, eg *whose*, *which*
- can be one of two types:

a. **defining relative clauses** form part of the noun group and are used to explain which person or thing you are talking about

b. **non-defining relative clauses** add extra information, but the sentence will make sense without them. They are separated by commas from the main clause

Grammar in practice

A Say whether the following are compound or complex sentences:

1 *He acquired his nickname when he was four years old.*

2 *I used to love going down to Gran's; so did everyone else in the street.*

3 *She looked at me, then shifted her gaze to Kathleen.*

4 *Let's go to a show, or have dinner in that new Thai restaurant.*

5 *I'll wait here until you've finished.*

B Identify the type of subordinate clause in the following complex sentences:

1 *I was late, so I had to apologize to everyone.*

2 *Nothing turned out the way I'd imagined.*

3 *They sell the machines at a low price in order to gain market share.*

4 *Although his intentions were good, he didn't succeed in convincing anyone.*

5 *It was more powerful than the bomb we dropped on Hiroshima.*

6 *She looked at me as if I had suggested something improper.*

7 *He was hired because he was a skilled translator.*

8 *I have to drive wherever my employer tells me to drive.*

9 *Stir over a low heat until the sugar dissolves.*

10 *We'd be better off if nuclear weapons were totally eliminated.*

C Identify the relative clauses in the following sentences and say whether they are defining or non-defining:

1 *The tunnel that leads down to the generators is brightly-lit.*

2 *There is little to attract tourists, least of all the weather, which is generally dreadful.*

3 *His first piano teacher was a woman named Frieda, who charged a dollar a lesson.*

4 *The menu planned by the caterers included a vegetarian option.*

5 *He was a man who always did what was expected of him.*

Word formation

This chapter looks at two of the ways words are formed in English: **derivation** and **compounding**.

The process of derivation involves taking the base form of a word and adding an **affix**. This may be a **prefix**, added to the beginning of a word, or a **suffix**, added to the end of the word. This process forms a new word, often one that has a different grammatical function from the word from which it is derived.

The process of compounding is the linking of two or more words, often from different word classes, to create a compound word.

Prefixes

In most cases, when you add a prefix to a word, the new word is of the same word class as the original.

Many prefixes are used to form opposites or negative forms, or words that mean 'against', 'bad', or 'without'. Some of these are *a-*, *anti-*, *contra-*, *counter-*, *de-*, *dis-*, *il-*, *im-*, *in-*, *ir-*, *mal-*, *mis-*, *non-*, *un-*.

Nouns:
efficiency, *in*efficiency; approval, *dis*approval; event, *non*-event; argument, *counter*argument; ability, *in*ability; practice, *mal*practice; understanding, *mis*understanding; smoker, *non*-smoker

Verbs:
approve, *dis*approve; pack, *un*pack; like, *dis*like; stabilize, *de*stabilize; behave, *mis*behave; judge, *mis*judge

WORD FORMATION

Adjectives:

logical, *il*logical; patient, *im*patient; happy, *un*happy; visible, *in*visible; moral, *a*moral; possible, *im*possible; adequate, *in*adequate; responsible, *ir*responsible

Adverbs:

truthfully, *un*truthfully; agreeably, *dis*agreeably

Some other prefixes are *ante-*, *arch-*, *bi-*, *bio-*, *co-*, *crypto-*, *demi-*, *di-*, *eco-*, *ex-*, *extra-*, *fore-*, *hemi-*, *inter-*, *intra-*, *macro-*, *mega-*, *micro-*, *midi-*, *mini-*, *mono-*, *multi-*, *neo-*, *out-*, *over-*, *para-*, *poly-*, *post-*, *pre-*, *pro-*, *pseudo-*, *re-*, *retro-*, *self-*, *semi-*, *sub-*, *super-*, *supra-*, *sur-*, *tele-*, *trans-*, *tri-*, *ultra-*, *under-*, *uni-*, *vice-*.

They have a wide variety of meanings, for example:

ante- means 'before' as in *ante*natal
bi- means 'two' as in *bi*centenary
co- means 'with' as in *co*-star
eco- means 'connected with the environment' as in *eco*system
ex- means 'former' as in *ex*-president
inter- means 'between' as in *inter*continental
mega- means 'extremely large', as in *mega*bucks
para- means 'similar' as in *para*medic
pro- means 'in favour of' as in *pro*-Western
re- means 'again' as in *re*appear
sub- means 'under' as in *sub*soil
trans- means 'from one side to the other' as in *trans*continental
ultra- means 'very' as in *ultra*-careful

Note that in some cases, if you remove a prefix, the resulting word cannot stand alone. For example *contradict* means 'to say something is untrue', but there is no word 'dict'. 'Dict' has a Latin root meaning 'say'. There are hundreds of words like this, eg *bigamy*, *antibiotics*, *antecedent*.

Suffixes

Some common suffixes are *-ability*, *-able*, *-age*, *-al*, *-ance*, *-ant*, *-ary*, *-bound*, *-cy*, *-dom*, *-ee*, *-en*, *-ence*, *-ent*, *-er*, *-ery*, *-ese*, *-fold*, *-ful*, *-gram*, *-graph*, *-head*, *-hood*, *-ian*, *-ibility*, *-ible*, *-ic*, *-ics*, *-ish*, *-ism*, *-ist*, *-ite*, *-itis*, *-ity*, *-ive*, *-ize*, *-kind*, *-less*, *-like*, *-ly*, *-mania*, *-ment*, *-minded*, *-most*, *-ness*, *-old*, *-ology*, *-ological*, *-ous*, *-phile*, *-proof*, *-related*, *-rich*, *-ship*, *-side*, *-size*, *-some*, *-speak*, *-stricken*, *-type*, *-ure*, *-wards*, *-wide*, *-wise*, *-work*, *-worthy*, *-y*.

When you add a suffix to a word, there may be spelling changes, for example a final *e* is often dropped, or a *y* changes into an *i*. Adding a suffix often, but not always, changes the word class that a word falls into. Here are some examples:

-able combines with verbs to form adjectives, eg admir*able*, avoid*able*.

-age combines with verbs, nouns and adjectives to form new nouns, eg marri*age*, short*age*.

-bound combines with nouns to form adjectives meaning that someone is restricted or limited in some way, eg house*bound*, desk*bound*.

-dom combines with nouns and adjectives to form new nouns meaning a state or condition, eg king*dom*, star*dom*.

-ee combines with verbs to form nouns referring to someone who is affected by an action, eg detain*ee*, train*ee*.

-er combines with verbs to form nouns referring to people who have a particular job, eg wait*er*, paint*er*.

-ful combines with nouns to form new nouns referring to measurements or adjectives referring to qualities, eg teaspoon*ful*, pain*ful*.

-hood combines with nouns to form new nouns which refer to a

state or a period of time in your life, eg nation*hood*, adult*hood*.

-ish has many meanings. For example, it combines with adjectives to form new nouns meaning 'fairly', eg small*ish*, tall*ish*.

-less combines with nouns to form adjectives meaning that someone or something is lacking something, eg power*less*, use*less*.

-ment combines with verbs to form nouns, eg develop*ment*, discourage*ment*.

-ness combines with adjectives to form nouns, eg happi*ness*, rude*ness*.

-ship combines with nouns to form new nouns, eg citizen*ship*, leader*ship*.

-y combines with nouns to form adjectives, eg dirt*y*, thirst*y*.

Compounds

The process of compounding produces compound words in a variety of classes. The elements which make up a compound do not necessarily belong to the same word class as the compound itself. Compounds usually have their own entries in dictionaries, though dictionaries differ widely in terms of what is considered to be a compound and what is considered to be just a frequent **collocation**.

A collocation is when two or more words are very often found near each other, like **apple** and **tree**, **narrow** and **margin**.

Compound nouns

A compound noun is a noun that is made up of more than one word and functions in a clause as a single noun. Compounds may be combinations of nouns with adjectives, verbs or other nouns. Some, like *bird of prey*, contain prepositions; some, like *cover-up*, contain adverbs, and a few, like *bride-to-be*, contain *to*-infinitives.

Some compounds are hyphenated, and some are written as two separate words. Some, like *brother-in-law*, consist of three words, and a few, like *lily of the valley*, have four. Again, dictionaries differ widely in this respect, and there are no hard and fast rules.

Some common compound nouns are *address book*, *air-conditioner*, *alarm clock*, *baby-sitter*, *back-seat driver*, *brother-in-law*, *come-on*, *common sense*, *contact lens*, *cost of living*, *death penalty*, *do-it-yourself*, *fast food*, *general knowledge*, *human being*, *income tax*, *looker-on*, *make-up*, *mother tongue*, *nervous breakdown*, *old age*, *package holiday*, *remote control*, *runner-up*, *science fiction*, *sign language*, *solar system*, *summing-up*, *swimming pool*, *T-shirt*, *washing-up liquid*, *yellow pages*.

The plurals of compound nouns are usually formed in the normal way by adding *-s* or *-es*, like *musical instruments* or *fire engines*. In a few cases, when the main noun comes first, this may be the element that pluralizes, eg *mothers-in-law*, *passers-by*, *courts of law*, *lilies of the valley*, *runners-up*.

Compound verbs

A compound verb is a verb that is made up of more than one word and functions in a clause as a single verb. Compound verbs are usually hyphenated, even if the related compound noun does not have a hyphen, eg *roller skate* (noun) and *roller-skate* (verb). Compound verbs are formed in a number of ways, usually using a noun plus a verb, eg *mass-produce*, *ice-skate*, *baby-sit*. A few have been borrowed from foreign languages, like *ad-lib*.

Some common compound verbs are *back-pedal*, *blow-dry*, *bottle-feed*, *breastfeed*, *chain-smoke*, *cold-shoulder*, *court-martial*, *cross-check*, *cross-examine*, *deep-fry*, *double-check*, *double-park*, *dry-clean*, *ghost-write*, *hitch-hike*, *ill-treat*, *lip-read*, *mass-produce*, *play-act*, *rubber-stamp*, *short-change*, *spin-dry*, *spoon-feed*, *stage-manage*, *stir-fry*, *touch-type*, *water-ski*, *window-shop*.

WORD FORMATION

Compound adjectives

A compound adjective is an adjective that is made up of more than one word and functions in a clause as a single adjective. Compound adjectives are usually hyphenated. They are formed in a number of ways, using:

- an adjective, an adverb or a number plus a noun plus *-ed*, eg *grey-haired*, *open-ended*, *high-powered*, *kind-hearted*, *one-sided*
- an adjective or adverb plus the *-ed* form of a verb, eg *low-pitched*, *high-priced*, *well-brought-up*, *well-placed*
- an adjective, adverb or noun plus the *-ing* form of a verb, eg *all-consuming*, *long-suffering*, *good-looking*, *man-eating*, *sea-going*, *soul-destroying*, *far-reaching*
- a noun plus the *-ed* form of a verb, eg *tongue-tied*, *wind-blown*
- a noun plus an adjective, eg *top-heavy*, *accident-prone*, *snow-white*, *colour-blind*
- an adjective plus a noun, eg *deep-sea*, *present-day*
- an *-ed* form plus an adverb, eg *run-down*, *cast-off*

Some common compound adjectives are *absent-minded*, *brand-new*, *big-headed*, *clear-cut*, *duty-free*, *easy-going*, *empty-handed*, *free-range*, *good-natured*, *high-heeled*, *home-made*, *laid-back*, *lead-free*, *low-paid*, *middle-aged*, *mouth-watering*, *narrow-minded*, *never-ending*, *off-putting*, *old-fashioned*, *open-minded*, *panic-stricken*, *part-time*, *record-breaking*, *short-handed*, *smooth-talking*, *so-called*, *starry-eyed*, *trouble-free*, *two-faced*, *well-dressed*, *worldly-wise*.

Compound adverbs

Compound adverbs are usually formed by adding *-ly* to compound adjectives, eg *absent-mindedly*, *cold-bloodedly*, *even-handedly*, *good-naturedly*, *kind-heartedly*, *mouth-wateringly*, *single-handedly*. Not many of the compound adjectives allow this.

Checklist

Derivation involves adding an affix (either a prefix or a suffix) to a word.

1. **Prefixes**
   - are added to the beginning of words and are usually of the same word class as the original, eg *anti-*, *contra-*, *in-*, *ir-*, *super-*, *ultra-*
   - cannot be removed from certain words, eg *antibiotics*

2. **Suffixes**
   - are added to the end of words, eg *-ability*, *-ful*, *-ism*, *-worthy*
   - often change the spelling of a word when they are added, eg *admire – admirable*
   - often change the word class of a word to which they are added, eg *trust* [verb] – *trustworthy* [adjective]

3. **Compounds**
   - are formed by linking two or more words, often of different word classes, eg *fast food*
   - can take the form of nouns, verbs, adjectives and adverbs

Grammar in practice

A Add a prefix to the following words to make a new word which is its opposite in some way, that is, it means 'against', 'bad' or 'without':

   1 *war*
   2 *advantage*
   3 *indication*
   4 *literate*

5 *espionage*

6 *conscious*

7 *regulate*

8 *obedient*

9 *practical*

10 *profitable*

11 *formal*

12 *management*

13 *function*

14 *legal*

15 *replaceable*

B Use the suffixes listed below to make new words. Say which word class the word was, and the word class you have formed:

-ship	-able	-ness	-al	-dom
-age	-ance	-ish	-ism	-less

1 *manage*

2 *gentle*

3 *store*

4 *friend*

5 *patriot*

6 *government*

7 *young*

8 *attend*

9 *harm*

10 *martyr*

Solutions

Parts of the clause

A 1 *The prison* – subject; *by the British* – adjunct; *early in the century* – adjunct

     2 *Four thousand men and women* – subject; *here* – adjunct

     3 *The lighthouse* – subject; *a wide blade of light* – object; *across the horizon* – adjunct

     4 *What* – object; *I* – subject; *there* – adjunct

     5 *What I wanted* – subject; *to get out of there* – complement

     6 *An hour later* – adjunct; *we* – subject; *to Canton* – adjunct; *up the estuary of the Pearl River* – adjunct

     7 *Canton* – subject; *at once the flashiest and most traditional of the great cities* – complement

     8 *Under the banyan trees* – adjunct; *youths* – subject; *bracelets and pocket calculators* – object

     9 *One of these multi-tiered restaurants* – subject; *snakes* – object

    10 *Then* – adjunct; *he* – subject; *silent* – complement [*fall* in this sentence is a link verb]

B 1 *her*

     2 *you*

     3 *the visitors*

     4 *me*

     5 *her*

C **1** *uncle*

2 *a compliment*

3 *a master of the art*

4 *dead*

5 *free and equal*

Nouns and noun groups

A *For <u>this recipe</u> <u>you</u> can use <u>any winter vegetables that are available</u>, for example <u>cauliflower</u>, <u>carrots</u> and <u>onions</u>. Start off by crushing <u>the cumin</u>, <u>coriander</u> and <u>mustard seeds</u> with <u>a pestle and mortar</u>. Then heat <u>the oil</u> in <u>a medium saucepan</u> and stir <u>the prepared vegetables</u> into <u>it</u>. Cook <u>them</u> over <u>a fairly high heat</u> until <u>they</u>'re lightly browned, stirring frequently. Then turn <u>the heat</u> down low and stir in <u>the crushed seeds</u>, <u>turmeric</u>, <u>cayenne</u>, <u>a seasoning of salt and pepper</u>, and finally <u>the yoghurt</u>.*

B **1** *answer* – count

2 *news* – uncount

3 *congratulations* – plural

4 *sheep* – count

5 *education* – count and uncount

6 *coffee* – count and uncount

7 *mainland* – singular

8 *grounding* – singular

9 *committee* – collective

10 *sunshine* – uncount

11 *decision* – count

12 *music* – uncount

13 *suicide* – count and uncount

14 *dreadlocks* – plural

15 *cleanser* – count and uncount

16 *hurry* – singular

17 *trousers* – plural

18 *electorate* – collective

19 *physics* – uncount

20 *livestock* -collective

Verbs and phrasal verbs

A   1 *ask* – transitive and intransitive

2 *pay* – transitive and intransitive

3 *melt* – ergative

4 *fight* – reciprocal

5 *become* – link

6 *disappear* – intransitive

7 *kill* – transitive and intransitive

8 *control* – transitive

9 *attack* – transitive and intransitive

10 *dance* – reciprocal

11 *laugh* – intransitive

12 *change* – ergative

13 *drive* – transitive and intransitive

14 *reverse* – ergative

15 *hear* – transitive and intransitive

16 *handle* – transitive

17 *throw* – transitive

18 *disagree* – reciprocal

19 *matter* – intransitive

20 *remove* – transitive

B 1 *give away, give back, give in, give off, give out, give over, give up*

2 *look after, look ahead, look around, look back, look down on, look forward to, look in, look into, look on, look out, look out for, look over, look round, look through, look to, look up, look upon, look up to*

3 *break away, break down, break in, break into, break off, break out, break through, break up*

4 *write back, write down, write in, write into, write off, write out, write up*

5 *talk back, talk down, talk down to, talk into, talk out, talk out of, talk over, talk round, talk through, talk up*

Verb tenses

A 1 *simple past*

2 *present perfect progressive*

3 *future perfect*

4 *future progressive*

5 *present perfect*

6 *simple present*

7 *past perfect progressive*

8 *present progressive*

9 *past perfect*

200

    10 *past progressive*

B   **1** *should* – modal

    2 *may* – modal
      [Note that in this sentence *have* is a main verb]

    3 *have* – auxiliary; *can* – modal

    4 *was* – auxiliary

    5 *'s* – contraction of auxiliary *is*

    6 *didn't* – auxiliary + *n't*

    7 *would* – modal; *don't* – aux + *n't*

    8 *must* – modal; *have* – auxiliary
      [Note that in this sentence *be* is a main verb]

    9 *could* – modal

    10 *was* – auxiliary; *might* – modal

More about verb groups

A   **1** *The company's goals <u>have</u> never <u>been achieved</u>.*

    2 *The game <u>cannot be cancelled</u> at this late stage.*

    3 *The painting <u>is owned</u> by a private collector.*

    4 *Mo <u>was</u> actually <u>christened</u> Julianne.*

    5 *A few months in a monastery <u>has been suggested</u>.*

B   **1** *was diagnosed*

    2 *has been run*

    3 *will be passed*

    4 *has been written/was written*

    5 *had been burnt*

C 1 *indicative*

2 *interrogative*

3 *imperative*

4 *subjunctive*

5 *interrogative*

Adjectives and adjective groups

A 1 *no*

2 *yes*

3 *yes*

4 *yes*

5 *yes*

B 1 *The night air was <u>cool</u> against her skin.*

2 *Birmingham is <u>famous</u> as the home of the industrial revolution.*

3 *Universities need to be more <u>involved</u> in student life.*

4 *Last year he was <u>absent</u> from work for 25 days.*

5 *She was <u>terrified</u> of heights.*

6 *I'm very <u>particular</u> about what I eat.*

7 *These plants attract many insects that are <u>beneficial</u> to the birds.*

8 *They were not <u>eligible</u> for government benefits.*

9 *My dad's not too <u>keen</u> on me going away.*

10 *I've always been <u>mean</u> with money.*

C 1 *We would be <u>foolish</u> to ignore their advice.*

2 *The garden was <u>beautiful</u> to look at.*

3 *I was* <u>puzzled</u> *to find all the doors locked.*

4 *I'd be* <u>interested</u> *to know what you think about it.*

5 *He was* <u>lucky</u> *to escape with his life.*

Adverbs, adverb groups and adjuncts

A 1 *Chocolate is the most* <u>commonly</u> *craved food.*

2 <u>*Recently*</u> *I have tried my hand at portrait painting.*

3 *We* <u>narrowly</u> *defeated the opposition.*

4 *Scientists have been working* <u>quietly</u> *behind the scenes.*

5 *Our married life continued* <u>happily</u> *for six years.*

6 *I went to the graveyard of my dearly loved and* <u>sadly</u> *missed husband.*

7 *Cook until tender or until a fork goes in* <u>easily</u>.

8 *You should drive very* <u>carefully</u> *in frosty weather.*

9 *The journal is published* <u>monthly</u>.

10 *I play the guitar, though not very* <u>well</u>.

B 1 *with some reluctance* – manner

2 *only rarely* – frequency

3 *financially* – aspect

4 *anxiously* – manner

5 *basically* – sentence adverb

6 *these days* – time

7 *everywhere* – place

8 *therefore* – linking

9 *from about noon to nine at night* – duration

10 *instead* – linking

Pronouns

A 1 *He always embarrasses <u>me</u> in front of my friends.*

   2 *Jane and Sue didn't like each other much; <u>they</u> were always quarrelling.*

   3 *Mum said she would let <u>us</u> play by ourselves.*

   4 *As for Jason, I've seen nothing of <u>him</u> since the funeral.*

   5 *Martha knew what <u>she</u> wanted and said so.*

B 1 *He looked at me quickly, his eyes meeting <u>mine</u>.*

   2 *If you take one of ours, we'll take one of <u>yours</u>.*

   3 *She wears glasses like Grace, but <u>hers</u> have steel rims instead of brown ones.*

   4 *Leopards can't change their spots, but butterflies can shed <u>theirs</u> with surprising ease.*

   5 *That galaxy is millions of light years away from <u>ours</u>.*

C 1 *His wife was Mary, a nurse, to <u>whom</u> he was absolutely devoted.*

   2 *He was the man <u>who</u> was responsible for the mistakes.*

      [or He was the man <u>that</u> was responsible for the mistakes.]

   3 *I made friends with a girl <u>whose</u> father ran the ice-cream stall.*

   4 *It was music the likes of <u>which</u> he had never heard in his life.*

   5 *I pray for a day <u>when</u> nuclear weapons will no longer exist.*

Determiners

A 1 *When we'd saved a little money, after the first few years, we bought the land for this house.*

2 *We talked about my family and hers, our friends and what they were doing.*

3 *I had enough time for a cup of tea and another slice of toast.*

4 *He had developed a habit of starting his answer to any question with the words 'Well, no … yes.'*

5 *I took several lungfuls of the clean, sweet air.*

6 *Cook the meat until browned on both sides.*

7 *There are some details that require much thought.*

8 *She knew all the answers to our questions.*

9 *In those days, a ten-minute walk would get you out of the city and into the wilds.*

10 *Within a few months the rector died, and Manning stepped into his shoes.*

B 1 *She's called you a few times today.*

2 *I had too much worry, and too little sleep.*

3 *Slice the meat and pour a little sauce over it.*

4 *Unfortunately there was little media coverage of this exciting event.*

5 *We met on one of your few trips to the library.*

6 *Thicken the mixture with flour and a little water.*

7 *There was never any vandalism and few cigarette butts were dropped on the floor.*

8 *The city was almost deserted and few people passed us in the street.*

9   *I had <u>little</u> choice but to agree.*

10   *We managed to sleep for <u>a few</u> hours.*

Prepositions and prepositional phrases

A   1   *It's hard to get a job <u>without</u> any qualifications.*

2   *What have you been doing out <u>in</u> this weather?*

3   *The building of new houses extends far <u>beyond</u> the city limits.*

4   *We need to protect ourselves <u>against</u> the threat of nuclear war.*

5   *Several families lost their homes <u>during</u> the fighting.*

6   *The train station is <u>opposite</u> the Grand Victoria Hotel.*

7   *He had all the tools he needed, <u>including</u> a circular saw.*

8   *Can the desired improvements be achieved <u>at</u> less cost?*

9   *I just want to lie down <u>for</u> a while.*

10   *There is not much <u>about</u> the place to attract tourists.*

B   1   *I live <u>in</u> Bristol, <u>on</u> Beech Road.*

2   *The village is <u>on</u> the road to Kidderminster.*

3   *He punched him <u>in</u> the eye and knocked him over.*

4   *Jo was wild <u>at</u> school, and dropped out <u>at</u> the age of 16.*

5   *She worked <u>in</u> a hotel during the school holidays.*

C   1   *We need to look <u>into</u> the possibilities of wind-generated electricity.*

2   *What lies* <u>behind</u> *such crimes is pure and simple greed.*

3   *These old fireplaces are hard to come* <u>by</u>.

4   *I have not entered* <u>into</u> *any financial agreements.*

5   *He was living* <u>on</u> *£600 a month.*

Conjunctions

1   *then* links three clauses. In the last clause, *she said* has been dropped.

2   *either ... or* links two prepositional phrases.

3   *but* links two clauses. In the second clause, *she's* has been dropped.

4   *or* links two clauses.

5   *then* links two clauses.

6   *and* links two clauses. In the second clause, *he* has been dropped.

7   *or* links two noun groups.

8   *yet* links two adverb groups.

9   *but* links two adjectives in the same noun group.

10 *yet* links two clauses, *neither ... nor* links two noun groups.

11 *and* links two noun groups, *but* links two clauses.

12 *or* links two clauses, the second *or* links two noun groups. In the second group, *weeks* has been dropped.

13 *and* links the last two of three adjective groups.

14 *and so* links two clauses. In the second clause *interested in reading it* has been dropped.

15 *but* links two clauses.

Numbers

A
1 *one-fifth* – fraction
2 *half* – fraction
3 *nine* – cardinal number
4 *seven* – cardinal number
5 *seventh, second* – ordinal numbers
6 *one-tenth* – fraction
7 *fifth* – ordinal number
8 *170* – cardinal number
9 *a third* – fraction
10 *three-quarters* – fraction

B
1 *these two primary considerations*
2 *six more like him*
3 *those first three years*
4 *four billion dollars*
5 *another twelve miles*

Clauses and sentences

A
1 *complex*
2 *compound*
3 *compound*
4 *compound*
5 *complex*

B
1 *so I had to apologize to everyone* – result clause

2 *the way I'd imagined* – clause of manner

3 *in order to gain market share* – purpose clause

4 *Although his intentions were good* – concessive clause

5 *than the bomb we dropped on Hiroshima* – clause of comparison

6 *as if I had suggested something improper* – clause of manner

7 *because he was a skilled translator* – reason clause

8 *wherever my employer tells me to drive* – place clause

9 *until the sugar dissolves* – time clause

10 *if nuclear weapons were totally eliminated* – conditional clause

C 1 *that leads down to the generators* – defining

2 *which is generally dreadful* – non-defining

3 *who charged a dollar a lesson* – non-defining

4 *planned by the caterers* – defining

5 *who always did what was expected of him* – defining

Word formation

A 1 *anti-war*

2 *disadvantage*

3 *contraindication*

4 *illiterate*

5 *counter-espionage*

6 *unconscious*

7 *deregulate*

8 *disobedient*

9 *impractical*

10 *unprofitable*

11 *informal*

12 *mismanagement*

13 *malfunction*

14 *illegal*

15 *irreplaceable*

B

1 *manageable* – verb to adjective

2 *gentleness* – adjective to noun

3 *storage* – verb to noun

4 *friendship* – noun to noun

5 *patriotism* – noun to noun

6 *governmental* – noun to adjective

7 *youngish* – adjective to adjective

8 *attendance* – verb to noun

9 *harmless* – noun to adjective

10 *martyrdom* – noun to noun

Index

Index

INDEX